GIRLS ALOUD

JEN CROTHERS

GIRLS ALOUD

THEY'RE STYLISH AND THEY'VE GOT ATTITUDE – THIS IS THE STORY OF BRITAIN'S BEST GIRL BAND

JOHN BLAKE

To Mum and Dad –
for believing in the five-year plan

Published by John Blake Publishing Ltd,
3 Bramber Court, 2 Bramber Road,
London W14 9PB, England

www.blake.co.uk

First published in paperback in 2007

ISBN: 978-1-84454-458-5

British Library Cataloguing-in-Publication Data:

A catalogue record for this book is available from the British Library.

Design by www.envydesign.co.uk

Printed in Great Britain by William Clowes Ltd, Beccles, Suffolk

1 3 5 7 9 10 8 6 4 2

Edited by Emily Sheridan
Researched by Susan Williams

Papers used by John Blake Publishing are natural, recyclable products made from wood grown in sustainable forests. The manufacturing processes conform to the environmental regulations of the country of origin.

Contents

	Preface	ix
	Introduction	xi
1.	Dancing Queen: Cheryl's Childhood	1
2.	Rock Chick in the Making: Sarah's Childhood	9
3.	Six Became Five: Nadine's Childhood	17
4.	Singing Sensation: Nicola's Childhood	29
5.	Acting Ambition: Kimberley's Childhood	35
6.	*Popstars: The Rivals*	41
7.	The First Year	67
8.	Cheryl in the Dock	89
9.	Nicola's Low-Key Loves	103
10.	Kimberley's Chemistry	109
11.	Nadine, the not-so-Desperate Housewife	115
12.	Sarah's Hunks (and Hack)	125
13.	Cheryl's Path to WAG-dom	135
14.	2004: What Will the Neighbours Say?	145

15. 2005: Girls on the Road 167
16. 2006: Keeping Pop Alive 195
17. Cheryl and Ashley Tie the Knot 227
18. 2007: The Greatest Hits 239
19. Love/Hate 251
Epilogue 271
Discography 275

Preface

30 NOVEMBER 2002 saw the birth of the most successful reality TV pop group in musical history. Five girls, Nadine Coyle, Cheryl Tweedy, Kimberley Walsh, Sarah Harding and Nicola Roberts were on the verge of making and breaking a barrage of records and winning the hearts of the nation – and would soon emerge as the UK's best girl group of recent years, Girls Aloud.

Lauded by many and loathed by few, the band would go on to succeed where other reality TV show-formed groups had failed, even managing to shed the 'talent show' stigma through hard work, bucketloads of attitude and an unprecedented reign over the Top 40 with a salvo of killer pop tunes – which earned them the respect of so-called 'proper music' critics and fans alike.

We look at the story behind the nation's favourite fivesome – the highs, the lows, and the combined sum of their parts which make Girls Aloud the true and rightful owners of their Princesses of Pop crown.

Introduction

BEFORE COMING TO prominence as Girls Aloud, Kimberley, Nicola, Nadine, Sarah and Cheryl were no strangers to the world of fame – a map of the well-trodden showbiz path was practically etched in the stars for each of the quintet. All worked hard for their place on the elusive train to stardom, dancing on national television, singing at local festivals and making up part of ill-fated and self confessed 'not very good' pop acts until career success finally came knocking.

In November 2002, they could finally reap the rewards of their childhood toils when they got the opportunity to stick a stiletto-heeled foot in the face of the UK music scene... little did pop know it would never be the same again.

But behind the fancy frocks and frills, the Girls Aloud story began with five very different tales spread across the northern regions of the British Isles...

CHAPTER 1

Dancing Queen: Cheryl's Childhood

CHERYL ANN TWEEDY was born in Heaton, Newcastle Upon Tyne, on 30 June 1983. She was the fourth child to join the Tweedy family, headed up by parents Joan Callaghan and Garry Tweedy – and it seems she was destined for fame since birth. Growing up in a council estate in a rough area of north east England did nothing to hamper young Cheryl, who had a happy childhood with older siblings Joseph, born in 1976; Andrew, born in 1980, and Gillian, born in 1979.

After Cheryl came to prominence with Girls Aloud in the closing stages of 2002, the *Daily Mail* claimed Cheryl 'did not come from a home where she was given many opportunities, and spent much of her young life dreaming of fame'. Dream of fame she did, but in truth, the right-wing paper sensationalised their pen portrait of the star in a January 2003 article, and would have been disappointed to report the young Ms Tweedy grew up with the wholehearted backing of parents Joan and Garry, who faithfully ferried the star-in-the-making to rehearsals, dance classes and castings week after week. 'When I decided I wanted to make a go of it as a singer, my mum spent a lot of time making my outfits and driving me about to the dance studios,' explains Cheryl.

Cheryl's success at such a young age was an indication of what was to come – lady luck would continue to smile at the petite Geordie throughout her formative years. As a tot, she was adorning her parents' mantelpiece with awards – still being in nappies didn't hold the determined youngster back. She won Boots The Chemist's Bonniest Baby contest, the baby paraphernalia retailers Mothercare's Happy Faces portrait competition, and *The Evening Chronicle*'s Little Miss and Mister search.

At four years old, Cheryl's desire to succeed shone through – the youngster knew she wanted to be a performer. Spurred on by her daughter's success as a beautiful child, mum Joan signed her up with a local modelling agency Pat Morgan, who recognised the future star's potential, with a burgeoning catwalk career even before she had started school: 'She won so many bonny baby competitions that a friend of mine suggested we took her to try out for modelling.' And it proved to be an astute move. 'She did loads for the Pat Morgan agency from the age of four, and went to shopping centres all over the place, strutting her stuff on the catwalks and stages,' says Joan.

The foundation stone on her path to stardom was

firmly laid by local paper the *Evening Chronicle* in 1990 when six-year-old Cheryl won the Star of the Future competition. Dressed to the nines in a frilly skirt, a flowery top and hair tousled into pigtails, Cheryl wowed the judges with her cute smile and inimitable charm, with judge Mike Whitehouse describing her as 'a little smasher'. Mum Joan fondly remembers the day Cheryl trounced the competition, adding the star was delighted to win £150 worth of vouchers for clothing chain Children's World: 'It was a lovely day. She really enjoyed herself. As a kid, that was her thing – dressing up and putting on a show. She has always been into clothes and when she won those vouchers she was thrilled because she got to buy loads more.'

The star would later be awarded top prizes in the Best Looking Girl of Newcastle contest, and was named the Most Attractive Girl at Gateshead's Metro Centre. This in itself was no mean feat – the centre is Europe's largest retail and leisure emporium. But Cheryl admits she was always desperate to be the centre of attention: 'I was always the show-off of the family, always wanting to do things and have my photograph taken.' And in 1987, a new arrival blessed the Tweedys – Cheryl was joined by a brother and modelling partner-in-crime, Garry.

While her peers were content to frolic in the playground and tend to their army of dolls, Cheryl was busy getting her face seen by the masses – namely in two television commercials for British Gas, the first of which she would appear in aged seven. Cheryl shared the screen with younger brother Garry in the advertisement, with the two Tweedys cavorting in the bath, and ultimately showing just how much fun it is to have a gas supply in the home. Mum Joan recalls, 'You could say she was a sort of soap star – in the bath. She was lovely even as a little girl and used to get lots of work. She was picked to star in the British Gas ad and was shot being washed by her screen mother in the bath. She isn't embarrassed about it because she was just a little girl. It proved she was a natural in front of the cameras.'

Her natural ability under the bright lights and pressure of television cameras was a skill that would stand her in very good stead for the future, and not just 12 years later when she enrolled in the *Popstars* talent circus. Cheryl and Garry would team up once again for an advertisement for Newcastle's Eldon Square shopping centre, with Cheryl going it alone in publicity for Sunderland-based furniture retailer SCS.

But it wasn't just about television appearances and cashing in on her good looks for Cheryl. Eager to pursue a career as a dancer, she enrolled as a pupil at the Newcastle Dance Centre aged 10, where she excelled in a wide range of dancing styles, including ballroom and ballet, while nurturing a love of music. 'I used to enter loads of dance competitions, and I wrote loads of songs,' she explains. Spurred on by her success and aptitude for dancing, Cheryl teamed up with a boy partner for the British Dance Championships and would later perform with him on Michael Barrymore's popular prime-time Saturday night TV programme *My Kind Of People* – almost a predecessor to the current crop of TV talent shows. People of all ages were offered the opportunity to get noticed in local shopping centres, where they would perform their talent or skill for an audience and Barrymore. The most successful were invited into the studio to reprise their performance.

Financially it was tough for the Tweedys, as painter and decorator dad Garry would work while mum Joan stayed at home to bring up the children – but they never let their daughter's dreams of stardom fade. 'There wasn't a lot of money,' explains Cheryl, 'but mum and dad always found enough for my audition outfits. My mum would take me to auditions. If I got a part, dad would shout, "Get in there" like a football fan, but all mum would say was, "Oh good." She will always keep my feet on the ground.'

A keen ballet dancer, Cheryl battled against 5000 fellow dance-mad kids to win a place at the Royal Ballet's summer school in London. Described by her ballet teacher Margaret Waite as 'a really exceptional dancer', Cheryl was one of the top ballerinas for her age. The youngster was delighted by her achievement, but it came at a tough time for the Tweedys – the family couldn't afford to send their younger daughter down south for the classes she had so set her heart on. But thanks to a local fundraising appeal, a sponsor kindly donated the £300 fees. Speaking at the time, Cheryl said, 'I'd like to thank them very much and I promise I will do my best.' Mum Joan added: 'It's fantastic that she's going to the ballet school. It would have broken Cheryl's heart if she had missed out.'

But Cheryl found the transition from the friendliness she knew in Newcastle to the constant hustle and bustle of London extremely difficult, and admits she was the black sheep of the young dancers chosen to participate in the summer school. She admits: 'I wanted to go home straight away. Everyone was prim and proper and I was just a Geordie from a council estate. Their parents all had money and we struggled just to get the cash to travel down to London. I felt that I was the odd one out. [At one of the performances] I was the only one waving to my mum, excited to see her.' When the two-week course finally came to an end, Cheryl was relieved, as she had spent the course feeling utterly homesick and teary-eyed – and the experience made her realise she didn't want to be a professional ballerina: 'It shattered my dream but I didn't want to have to stand a certain way all my life and only eat salad.' The epiphany meant dancing's loss was to be pop's gain – but little Cheryl wasn't to know it would perhaps be the best decision she ever made.

Safely back home in Newcastle, Cheryl started the new school term afresh, and was a popular and outgoing pupil at Walker Comprehensive, which she attended from the age of 11. Staff at the school were quick to recognise the youngster's talent, and soon realised they were lucky enough to be nurturing Heaton's soon-to-be most famous daughter. Dr Steve Gater, Cheryl's headmaster, recalls, 'It was obvious early on that Cheryl was ambitious and talented. From a young age her passions were singing and dancing. The staff didn't anticipate how big she would become but clearly the potential was there. She stood head and shoulders above everybody else. She loved being centre stage. Once she gave a speech to 250 kids for a Christmas Box appeal and was so good that a letter of commendation was sent to her parents.' Saying 'the staff didn't realise Cheryl's potential' may have been a thinly veiled euphemism for something else, as Cheryl had a different story to tell about her childhood days. 'I was awful,' she says. 'They used to throw me out of the class. My headmaster said to me, "It will be interesting to see what you do with your life, Miss Tweedy."'

Soon music took over as Cheryl's first love, and at 12 years old she was signed up by a management company. From the age of 14, she began travelling to London where she tried to make a name for herself on the music scene, knocking on record company doors to drum up interest in her vocal talent. Cheryl knew she wanted to be a success. 'I would watch [TV music shows] and things like that,' she says, 'and actually feel I could be physically sick with just wanting to be up there – nothing to do with the fame side of it really, just the performance side of it.' She worked as a session singer, but with her daughter 270 miles away from home, Joan couldn't help but be apprehensive about Cheryl in the Big Smoke: 'We always encouraged her, but when she was singing as a session vocalist in London I would worry about her being on her own.' But Cheryl's independence and determination to succeed shone through, and she caught the attention of a DJ, The Artful Dodger, with whom she recorded some tracks, and managed to continue touring the pub and club circuit in her spare time.

After leaving school at 16, Cheryl returned to the Newcastle Dance Centre for help with choreographing dance routines. Michael Conway, the centre's principal, explains, 'Cheryl always wanted to be a star. She had charisma and lots of talent but she also worked very hard to learn her routines. Everyone here is proud of what she's achieved.' But Cheryl's dad was fearful for his daughter's future after she dropped out of school. '[She] had that drive, although I used to tell her to get something to fall back on, like exams.'

She took a job as a cocktail waitress at Newcastle boat-based nightclub the Tuxedo Princess – a bar which lists floating on the Tyne river as its unique selling point. With this, she juggled a series of solo singing stints somewhere which was no stranger to her talents – the Metro Centre, and the local pub and club circuit. She had been signed to Nikki Chapman's management company Brilliant, attending hundreds of auditions and showcases in her attempt for stardom. But it wasn't long before a 19-year-old Cheryl would put her vocal skills on a bigger platform than she could ever have imagined, when she submitted an application to a new talent show – *Popstars: The Rivals.*

CHAPTER 2

Rock Chick in the Making: Sarah's Childhood

SARAH NICOLE HARDMAN was born on 17 November 1981 in the Heatherwood Hospital in Ascot, Berkshire, the first child to parents John and Marie after her mother's son David, 16 years Sarah's senior. Even at birth, Sarah had music running through her veins, thanks to her dad, and would later use her experience to fulfil her destiny.

The angelic-looking blonde child had entered a musical dynasty – dad John was an acclaimed guitarist, songwriter and producer since the 1970s with rock band Sunfighter, and later worked with other musicians to perfect their sound. In 1986, he formed the group Beats Working, and was active in the music business throughout Sarah's childhood. Naturally, she nurtured a love of music early in life, with her dad introducing her to singing at age three in his music studio. 'I grew up with rock music, so I think it's great,' she would later tell music bible the *NME*. 'When I was little I used to go to gigs and get up and jam with my dad's band,' she says. 'As far back as I can remember, me and my brother were always singing – my poor mother! My mum would take me to his daytime gigs, and as I got older, I'd get up and sing along.' From a young age, Sarah would spend her days bouncing on the bed and singing along to Abba into a hairbrush. A few years later she had graduated to singing along to British musical institution Sir Cliff Richard, cradling one of her father's electric guitars in her arms. Within months, she knew all the words to her first album, Michael Jackson's iconic *Bad*, and would accompany the King of Pop in Staines via her hairbrush.

While her dad would be composing songs and writing lyrics for his band, mum Marie worked in a local office. Sarah attended a local school, and spent her spare time singing and performing for the rest of the family. They moved to Stockport in Greater Manchester when Sarah was 14 in 1996. She had a largely happy childhood until her mid-teens, when it was discovered John was having an affair with a younger woman. Music and drama teacher Katy Blackhurst was just roughly the same age as John Hardman's youngest daughter, and Sarah found her dad's behaviour hard to cope with. Sarah's parents' marriage of almost 30 years broke up, with the pair divorcing in 2001. Marie had been married and divorced twice before she wed Hardman, but the pain of the split was just as raw as it had been the first time. However, John would later claim he and Marie 'had drifted apart long before anyone else came on the scene'. He cited the age gap between him and Marie as difficult. Sarah later said, 'Mum and dad split up when I was 17. He went off with someone the same age as me.' The understandably acrimonious break-up saw the devastated teenager change her surname from Hardman to Harding to distance herself from the painful memory as much as possible – and reckoned 'Harding' was a much more showbiz name than her former moniker.

An unsettled Sarah attended Hazel Grove High in Stockport until the age of 15, but dropped out prior to sitting her GCSE exams to follow her dream of being a performer – and undoubtedly the pain of her parent's separation had taken its toll, manifesting itself in her bad behaviour. Frustrated at being forced to take English, maths and science classes instead of drama, headstrong Sarah took matters into her own hands and waved goodbye to full time education in 1997. She explains, 'I didn't see the point in doing GSCEs I wasn't interested in. I said, "Listen, if you want me to take my classes, I'm doing Performing Arts." But they wouldn't let me have a tutor so I just went off and got a job. If it didn't involve a textbook, I was happy.'

The singer knew leaving school so early without any recognised qualifications was a dangerous move, as she was now bound to pursuing her singing career, but remained defiant, 'You don't need qualifications to prove that you are intelligent.' However even today, she is not entirely comfortable dragging up the details of her days as a schoolgirl. But Sarah is the first to admit she was a badly behaved youth, often playing truant from Hazel

Grove and getting up to all kinds of mischief: 'I was a reprobate as a teenager, and there are certain times you go off the rails.' She says, 'I don't really like to talk about that part of my life because it's not something I really want to flag up,' but admits, 'It was my dream and I knew it was a big risk. I'm quite stubborn and I just wanted to do Performing Arts full time.'

However, aged 16 Sarah almost fell into a debilitating downward spiral of drug-taking. Troubled by her parents' then-rocky marriage, she turned to cannabis to help ease the pain. Speaking to the *News Of The World* in 2003, she explained her drug use following the beginning of her parents' marriage difficulties for two years until the age of 18. She said, 'I started hanging around with the wrong crowd, drinking heavily just trying to block out the pain of my parents splitting up. One night after work we went to a mate's house and carried on drinking, then someone passed me a joint. I'd never touched anything like that before but I thought, "Who cares?" and took a drag.'

Sarah admitted she relied on cannabis when times got tough with her nascent singing career: 'I was doing a lot of gigs around the area, singing in clubs, but my life was going nowhere. I'd been given all these false promises by people who said they'd help me. So I started smoking it whenever I could. I knew what it did to me and I liked it because I could forget every that was crap around me.' Luckily Sarah soon had an epiphany, realising the drugs weren't helping her come to terms with what was happening around her and kicked the habit at 18-years-old. 'My darkest time in Stockport is now a distant memory,' she explains. 'One morning I just thought, What am I doing with my life? Thinking about it now I can't believe what I was doing. No matter what happens in your life, turning to drugs won't help. You should talk to someone. Things are never so bad you have to do something that will harm your body.'

Sarah concedes the move up north wasn't as bad as it seemed, as it was here that she began attending Performing Arts classes at North Cheshire Theatre College after her departure from school. She admits, 'I had some good fun in Stockport. Stockport is where my life really began. It's where I started going to Performing Arts three times a week. My parents didn't have a lot of money and could only afford to send me once a week down south. From the age of 11 I went to drama school; I was always on at my mum and dad to send me to somewhere like Italia Conti, but they couldn't afford it.'

Sarah knew that making it in the entertainment industry wouldn't pay the bills until she really hit the big time, and juggled a brief career in hairdressing after completing a National Vocational Qualification (NVQ) at higher education establishment Stockport College, as she knew she would then have something to fall back on if her singing didn't work out. After a short stint in a salon, she was taken under the wing of a music producer who helped land the youngster gig bookings in clubs and pubs in Wales. 'At 17 I got a manager and started gigging around Rhyl in Wales,' she recalls. 'I'd sing two 45-minute sets, then drive all the way home.' Spurred on by her success on the circuit, she helped form local Stockport pop act Project G, spending her spare time laying down vocals and participating in promotional photoshoots. Sarah was disappointed when nothing ever came of Project G, but remained upbeat about what lay ahead.

Sarah's good looks and friendly demeanour helped her to land a job promoting local nightclub Volts in Stockport alongside future local radio host Chelsea Norris. Hard-working Sarah took on more employment, with a CV more varied than most; acting as a waitress in Pizza Hut and a barmaid in Manchester, a telephone operator on British Telecom's 192 Directory Enquiries service, a debt collector and even a van driver – but her desire for stardom never faltered. She saw an advert in lads mag *FHM* for their annual High Street Honeys contest, in which members of the public are urged to send in pictures of local aesthetic talent in their town – or the girls themselves can send in a picture. Proud of her perfectly toned and tanned body, Sarah decided she was in with a good chance of winning – and any press coverage on the back of her entry would help raise her profile. Draped in a St George's flag for the revealing shot, Sarah popped the saucy pictures in the post and hoped for the best... but it was to be a photography session the star would soon live to regret. 'That was just me trying to get some profile,' she says. 'It worked.'

She never gave up hope she would soon be hitting the big time, and in August 2002, the news that a new TV talent show was searching for the biggest British girl band since the Spice Girls filled a 20-year-old Sarah with delight – it was just the break she had been waiting for. Marie urged her daughter to attend the auditions, as she was confident Sarah had what *Popstars: The Rivals* was looking for. A desire to make her mother proud was at the forefront of Sarah's mind. Marie was keen to see her daughter realise her dreams, and would religiously taxi Sarah to her gigs miles away in North Wales.

A former Project G bandmate got in touch just before the auditions, and the pair decided to queue overnight to be in with a chance of being seen by the judges: 'I used to be in a band and one of my friends, who was also in the band, rang me the night before the open auditions and asked me if I wanted to do it. I thought I had nothing to lose so we camped out overnight. I never thought I'd get past the first stage' – although she admits she was slightly apprehensive about that particular path into the music industry. 'In the past I've had some bad experiences and had my heart broken,' she explained. 'So when a friend told me about the programme, I said, "You're joking, aren't you?" – I didn't want to make a fool of myself on television.' Undeterred, on 16 August 2002, Sarah headed to the swanky five-star Lowry Hotel in Manchester to impress the judges armed with her talent, good looks and determination.

CHAPTER 3

Six Became Five: Nadine's Childhood

NADINE ELIZABETH LOUISE Coyle was born on 15 June 1985 in Derry, Northern Ireland to parents Niall and Lillian. She was the couple's second daughter, after they welcomed Charmaine into the family eight years earlier.

The then-youngest Coyle already had a lot to live up to and a destiny to fulfil – if a local fortune teller was to be believed. Her mother had been told as a teenager she would have three children – with the second-born infant destined for stardom: 'When I was 15 I went to this fortune teller, so she told me I would have three girls and that my middle daughter was going to be famous, so Nadine actually grew up believing she was going to be famous,' explains Lillian. Growing up in a tight-knit family with music and drama at its centre, Nadine was well versed in the art of performing from a very early age – and impressed her family with her singing talents as a tot. 'I remember the very first time I heard Nadine singing,' recalls Lillian. 'She was only two and sitting in the back seat of my car. She broke into 'Saturday Night At The Movies' and from that point, we knew she had an amazing voice.' Her father was an actor and popular local singer, and immediately realised his daughter's vocal talent when she first opened her mouth to sing – but was keen to let her voice shape itself rather than coax the child into singing lessons or coaching. He explains. 'I had some voice training, but as she got older, I didn't want Nadine to have the same because she had a very distinctive natural sound and capability.'

Nadine enrolled at St Patrick's Primary School in Pennyburn, Derry, where the teachers confirmed her parents' thoughts – she was an extremely talented youngster. Primary Three teacher Sister Anne had witnessed the youngster's talent in action, and urged parents Niall and Lillian to enter her into an esteemed local festival. So, at six years old, Nadine made her debut public performance at the Derry Feis, a famous five-day celebration of Irish music and culture. Nadine impressed the judges so much that she triumphed over much older competitors with more mature voices in singing competitions. Her grandfather, war veteran John Kavanagh, was so proud of his granddaughter's voice, he recorded Nadine singing in the traditional Irish Sean Nos – meaning unaccompanied – style on his old tape machine. Nadine was extremely close to her elderly grandfather. Speaking during the *Popstars* auditions, Nadine confessed she phoned him all the time for a chat and to ask how he was. Housewife Lillian gave birth to daughter Rachael in 1988, completing the Coyle sister triumvirate and providing another family member to participate in family-centric amateur dramatics.

At Christmas, local pantomimes were something of a family affair. Niall would produce and direct the plays, while the three Coyle sisters would tread the boards together. A young Nadine kept the fortune teller's words close to her heart, and was sure she would fulfil the now-fabled prophecy. Lillian says, 'Because of what I was told, I joked with Nadine when she was growing up that she was going to be famous.' Nadine was very close to her mother, treating her more like a friend than a parent. She says, 'I have a brilliant relationship with her. You know how some kids are scared of discussing things with their mum – I've never been like that. There's never been a time where I've not been able to go to her with a problem. She's always encouraged me, whether it was at school or with my singing. But she's never put any pressure on me to succeed.'

For Nadine, singing and performing was always a huge part of her life – and spurred on by her mother's words of wisdom, she was convinced she would fulfil the fortune teller's prophecy. 'Singing is the love of my life – it's what I live for.' she says. 'I've been singing since I was a kid and I would be running around the house when I was seven telling everyone I was going to be famous. As soon as I would finish school I would rush home and sing. Whenever I got the chance I also went into the recording studio and got experience.'

Aged 11, Nadine moved on to Thornhill College in Derry, attended by the city's most famous daughter – thus far – Eurovision legend Dana. But her thoughts didn't rest with her studies, as she put more effort into her dramatic pursuits. While her friends were busy planning for their future education, choosing which GCSEs they would study before embarking on A Levels and degree courses, Nadine didn't see the need to make provisions for her life after school – as she was confident her singing career would negate the need for a more conventional job. She says, 'Even at school, when they were planning for university, I would always think, "Why?" Sure I'm going to be a singer, why do I need to do that?' At 13 she appeared in local short film, *Surfing With William*, about a girl desperate to find her Prince Charming. Nadine's lack of interest in her education worried her parents – but knew she was the type of girl who had a knack for achieving when it really mattered the most. 'I remember being worried when it got close to her GCSEs because she had done absolutely no work,' explains Niall. 'Even when school gave her a week off to study she spent it in a studio recording a demo CD. That's where her heart was. But in typical Nadine fashion when her results came in, she had pulled it off again. She jumped on the bed and read out her results and it was 'A,B,B,B,A'. Her mum couldn't believe it. She actually rang the school to make sure there wasn't a mistake as her results were so good.'

In the autumn of 2001, 16-year-old Nadine got wind of a new reality TV show taking place in Ireland – a local version of ITV series *Popstars*. The successful band would be managed by Simon Cowell; as everything he touched had turned to gold in the past, for the winners, chart success was almost guaranteed. Three boys and three girls would be chosen for the line up – and fingers crossed they would soar to the dizzy heights of fame reached by that other Irish pop export, Westlife. It was the opportunity of a lifetime for Nadine and was too good to miss, but there was a catch. Applicants had to be 18 or over, and Nadine was two years short of the minimum age. Undeterred, she took her chances against 5,000 other hopefuls looking for their big break across Ireland, with auditions in Galway, Belfast, Cork and Dublin in September. Irish Eurovision Song Contest star Linda Martin, TV producer Bill Hughes and Irish pop mogul Louis Walsh would decide who had the talent to succeed, and who didn't. Louis was confident of the band's success, boasting, 'The band is going to be everywhere – like pollution. We are launching a new product and it will be out there in peoples' faces.'

Luckily for Nadine, she was one of the 32 young singers chosen to attend a rigorous week of vocal and dance coaching in Portumna in the West of Ireland. After the seven days of intense pop-star training was up, 20 wannabes' dreams of fame would end. Unsurprisingly, Nadine's talent shone through, and she made it to the final 12. From here on in, it was up to the Irish public to decide whether Nadine had what it takes to make up one sixth of a successful pop group.

The young Nadine, with her good looks and

breathtaking voice won over the hearts of the viewers, who voted for her in their droves. After months of uncertainty, the band's final line-up was announced – and Nadine had made the cut. She joined Andy Orr, Emma O'Driscoll, Liam McKenna, Sinead Shepard and Kyle Anderson in the newly formed band. Ireland's sextet of new stars moved into a luxury house in Ireland in preparation for their trip to the top of the charts, but it wasn't long before things began to unravel for Nadine. In a TV interview just 24 hours after moving into the new house together, the six members of Six were asked their date of births. Each one replied in turn, although under the pressure of the cameras, Nadine blew her own cover by rhyming off her date of birth, as she was used to doing outside of *Popstars*, as 15 June 1985 – she had been telling herself to say 1983, which would have made her the required age of 18. As soon as the mistake was made, she tried to correct herself: 'What date of birth did I give again?'

Nadine pleaded with producers it had been a slip up and she was in fact 18. But it was too late; the damage had been done and she later broke down off-camera and admitted her real age. TV bosses were shocked by the error, as Nadine had been a clear favourite during the show's run. Despite pleading with the judges and producers, and protestations from her fellow bandmates to keep the 16-year-old, bosses decided Nadine's breach of the rules meant she should be ousted from the band. The devastated teen said a tearful goodbye to her new friends, and was soon replaced by *Popstars* finalist Sarah

Keating. Producer Lynda McQuaid said, 'Nadine certainly doesn't look 16. To be honest, I just thought she'd made an error. I really did think that she'd stumbled. But, everytime I went, 'She's just made a mistake,' everybody would go, 'You don't get your date of birth wrong.' It is a sad tale and I'm very sorry for Nadine, but none of what happened on the programme detracts from the fact that she is a phenomenal talent.'

The show was aired two months after the initial series of events had unfolded, and Nadine suspected the controversy would continue when the episode hit TV screens in January. Given time to reflect on the scale of what had happened, Nadine became angry. She says, 'To be honest, I think it was cruel what they done to me.' Niall agreed with his daughter, and told the local press: 'Nobody but Nadine and ourselves know how that affected her, but the whole story about that never came out. As I watched it I did not think it was handled sensitively.' Lillian added: 'Nadine was totally shocked. She loved every single one of those people and it just hurt her to see the way they treated her in return.'

In January 2002, Nadine's 'lie' was to shock the TV-viewing public on the island of Ireland, subsequently shattering her dreams of fame and fortune. Commentators and local celebrities alike lined up to criticise the star, who was understandably devastated the chance to be in a pop group had slipped from her grip. The show's producer, Lynda McQuaid, later lambasted Nadine for lying her way onto the show, and dismissed reports the Derry girl had been the catalyst for Irish

Popstars' success. She says, 'I don't think it's fair to say Nadine made our series – it would have been just as successful without her. Her lie paid off, which I think is very unfortunate. She was the only one who lied and she's the only one of the finalists who has realised her dream. Life's not supposed to be like that.' But Nadine hit back, pointing out that as a 16-year-old – at least two years younger than her *Popstars* counterparts – she lacked the experience of her fellow auditionees: 'I was cheating myself, rather than anybody else, because cheating is giving yourself an unfair advantage over everybody else. And what I done was disadvantage myself, by at least two years.' But Irish *Popstars* judge Linda Martin would later leap to Nadine's defence, branding the episode the best thing that ever happened to Nadine: 'Every major star has lied or done things to get to the top.'

Adding insult to injury after the public lambasting over her painful exit from *Popstars*, Nadine could only look on as her former band Six made it to the top of the Irish charts in February 2002, with the fastest-selling single in Irish chart history with 'Whole Lot Of Loving'. But ever the team player to the end, she insisted she was pleased for the band: 'I hope that the band have the best success ever, because they are all lovely people. I really like every single one of them. If it had been different, if I had been 18, I would like to have still been in the band. But I'm not and there is no way it can be changed.' Despite the pain, Nadine told an RTE documentary on the Six scandal in 2007 she was thankful how events shaped up. 'I did do the wrong thing, but given the same chance, I would do it again.'

Louis Walsh was confident Nadine would still carve out a career in the music world, regardless of the Six debacle. He admitted her 'diva-esque' voice was far more mature than her years, saying, 'There's a big, long-lasting career out there for her in the pop world and she's going to be massive.'

While it looked like Nadine's singing star was on the rise, sadly, her dramatic exit from *Popstars* was to have a devastating effect on the rest of her family. The Coyles rallied to ignore the taunts aimed at Nadine together as a family, but sadly, it was youngest sibling Rachael who would be forced to suffer the price of her sister's fame – much to distraught Nadine's sorrow. Cruel bullies in Derry saw Rachael as an easy target – their view was that as her sister had suffered the shame of being ousted from *Popstars,* they could intimidate members of the Coyle family. Just 14 at the time, the bullying attacks triggered Bells Palsy in Rachael – a condition which paralyses muscles in the face.

Nadine remained hopeful about eventually hitting the big time, and was attracting interest from record companies wanting to sign her for a solo deal. 'Singing is still what I want to do and hopefully it's going to happen for me – sooner rather than later,' she said in March 2002. 'I've been talking to record companies and I've had a lot of offers. The interest has been amazing. I spent a few weeks in London but I can't say who's offered what yet. I still have some major decisions to make but it's looking good.' Nadine admitted she wanted to perform on her own – but, luckily for her future career path, conceded she would consider joining a band: 'I think I'd like to stick on my own now, although if there was a band out there looking for a singer, I wouldn't say no. It's all up in the air at the moment, but as long as I get to sing and perform, that's the main thing.'

In an unimaginable twist of fate, ITV's edition of *Popstars* was recruiting for new talent a little over six months since Nadine's first taste of the TV talent franchise. Although she was desperate to launch her singing career, she wasn't sure *Popstars* was the right platform from which to launch her to the British public after having her fingers well and truly burnt during Irish *Popstars*. But fate intervened, and the sister of her boyfriend, Charlton Athletic footballer Neil McCafferty, expressed her desire to enter the competition. Clare McCafferty was a dancer, but wanted to try out for the girl band which would be created by the show. Nadine agreed to help her perfect her singing, and undertook the 226-mile journey from Derry, across the Irish Sea to Glasgow in August 2002 to lend some moral support.

When the auditions finally began, nerves got the better of Clare and Nadine stepped in to take her place. Niall and Lillian had suggested she enter the competition herself, but knew ultimately, the decision was Nadine's. Lillian says, 'Nadine wasn't sure about entering but we really encouraged her as she is a fantastic singer. When a friend told her she was entering *Popstars: The Rivals,* Nadine offered to coach her and go to

Glasgow with her for the heats. When she left home that morning she had no intention of going for it. It was only after meeting some old friends from the Irish show that she changed her mind.' Despite the impending second shot at fame, Niall's words helped Nadine remain level-headed: 'I have told Nadine she has a fabulous gift and a unique vocal talent, but it is a gift from God. She cannot take credit for having that voice but she does have the responsibility to do something with it, and I am very proud of how she is handling that responsibility.' A level-headed and realistic Nadine wasn't bothered about the fame – she just wanted to be a revered singer. She admits, 'All you're doing is singing a song. You're not saving someone's life.'

Nadine's past experience of reality TV talent shows had left a bitter taste in her mouth, but always the consummate career-minded professional, the singer vowed to seize her second opportunity for stardom. She says, 'I wasn't going to go to the auditions after my experience in Irish *Popstars*. I just thought I would do nothing like that ever again. My confidence was so low. But I love singing and you only live once. Neil's sister is a dancer and she wanted to have a go at singing. So I just went along to the audition to give her support. When it came to the audition she said she couldn't do it. So I went into the room to sing.'

The chance participation in auditions for a TV show which had ended in tears once before was a brave decision for Nadine to make. All she could do now was wait for the phone to ring...

CHAPTER 4

Singing Sensation: Nicola's Childhood

NICOLA MARIA ROBERTS was born on 5 October 1985 to Debbie and Paul Roberts in Stamford, Lincolnshire. Her parents were delighted by the arrival of their first child, just a little over a year since their marriage, and decided to move back to their childhood home of Runcorn, Cheshire, to bring up Nicola and their future children.

Nicola, who was 17 years later to become the youngest member of Girls Aloud, was soon joined by younger sister Francesca Hope in May 1989. Seven years on saw the birth of little brother Harrison James in November 1996, with youngest brother Clayton George following in December 1999 – and due to the growing Roberts family, Debbie and Paul extended their semi-detached home to make room for the brood. Growing up in Runcorn, Cheshire, Nicola was very close to her family – especially sister Frankie, who at four years her junior was a ready-made playmate.

She attended Holy Spirit Primary School, where Debbie worked as a dinner lady, and was a popular but quiet child. It was while still at school, Nicola was to experience what she would later deem her most embarrassing moment – she went to a fancy dress party resplendently festooned with balloons to look like a bunch of grapes. She says, 'When I was little I wanted to enter a fancy dress contest. So my mum painted my face green, blew up lots of balloons and stuck them to me and I went as a bunch of grapes.' Dressing up as a piece of fruit didn't leave too many emotional scars for Nicola, who happily worked hard at Holy Spirit and, according to her teachers, was a gifted child.

Nicola's vocal talent came to the attention of her family aged 11, when she performed at family parties and engagements, wowing audiences with her musical ability – and like many pop stars in the making before her, it all started with a hairbrush masquerading as a microphone. Mum Debbie explains, 'She always sang with a hairbrush. Since she was 11, she said there is nothing else she wanted to do. I think fate has got a lot to do with it. If something's meant for you, it will happen. Nicola stunned guests at a dinner party when she sang a rendition of 'Everybody's Talking' while still at primary school. 'When we heard her we were amazed, she was only about 11,' says Debbie. At the height of the Spice Girls fame in the mid-1990s, Nicola found herself inspired by a high-profile fellow flame-haired female, and masterminded a mean Geri Halliwell karaoke routine. Little was she to know her success would soon eclipse that of the Spice Girls, and that she was soon to pilfer Ginger Spice's crown as the most famous redhead in British pop. Without a history of musically-minded relatives in the family, Nicola admits she's still baffled as to where she found her singing voice: 'My mum is tone deaf so I've no idea where my voice comes from.' But she admits she was full of self belief as a child, and would pester her parents about her future achievements. 'I used to say to my mum, "I wanna be a pop star when I grow up," and they'd be like, "Yeah, yeah, okay, okay."'

In September 1997, Nicola enrolled at the St Chads Catholic High School in Halton, regarded to be one of the best in the North West by school inspectors Ofsted, who branded it 'a good school with many outstanding features'. At the school she gained 10 GSCEs, before leaving to study for a B'TEC qualification in Performing Arts at Halton College (now known as Riverside College Halton following an amalgamation of Widnes & Runcorn Sixth Form College and Halton College), which stood her in good stead for the series of *Popstars: The Rivals* auditions which were to follow. Growing up, she and sister Frankie were extremely close – with the younger Roberts girl hoping to emulate her sister's success: 'Nicola's younger sister, Francesca, has got a lovely voice and is learning to dance,' explains Debbie. 'They have always had the same interests. She hopes to follow in Nicola's footsteps.'

Like several of her soon-to-be bandmates, Nicola

was working as a waitress before hitting the big time and auditioning for *Popstars: The Rivals*. The then 17-year-old Nicola had a part-time job at the Railway Pub in Runcorn as a waitress for a paltry £3.75 an hour. Working close to home was perfect for the youngster, as she is extremely close to her siblings and her parents. '[My mum and I] have everything in common and we look so alike people often mistake us for sisters. We often go shopping together because we like the same clothes.' Nicola is the first to admit her family come first in her life, and isn't keen to abandon her roots or stray far from her younger siblings: 'It's quite important for me to spend time with them because I don't want to be one of those sisters they don't see or don't know.'

'I want them to know me and feel like I'm part of the family – I'd hate to never be there. I don't want to be one of those sisters when they say, "There's Nicola, we saw her about twice when we were growing up." I don't want to not see them, so of course I'm going to go home whenever I can.'

Coming from such a large close-knit family had its benefits for Nicola growing up, and she would spend a lot of time with grandparents Eileen and Tom Trillingham; and Barbara and Gordon Roberts. From the very beginning of her granddaughter's rise to fame, proud Eileen began collecting all kinds of Girls Aloud paraphernalia, from CDs and DVDs to posters – with the couple's Cheshire home boasting signed Girls Aloud posters adorning the hallway. But long before her grandparents became Girls Aloud superfans, there was still a long way to go for Nicola. Every year, the Roberts' would spend their summer at a caravan in Devon, which Nicola highly enjoyed, even paying visits to her siblings and her dad at the caravan park when she became famous.

When she was younger, Nicola had formed a band with friends called Devotion, but nothing could match the potential kudos of being selected to be a singer in a new TV programme. Nicola heard about the new *Popstars: The Rivals* series, and was desperate to audition. This was her big chance to emulate her hero, Geri Halliwell, and so she mentioned to her mum she was going to phone up for an application form. 'No need!' cried Debbie, as, confident of her daughter's vocal talents, had got wind of the upcoming auditions and applied to the series without telling Nicola. She says, 'We obviously think alike, because she was the one who rang up to get me the *Popstars* application form. I heard about it and was going to apply but she said there was no need - she'd already done it for me.'

Weeks later, Nicola got a callback and was invited to audition for a place in a new girl band formed on *Popstars: The Rivals*. Nicola's dad Paul was delighted by his eldest daughter's success, but admits he would have been equally as happy if she had chosen something other than the stardom career path she had chosen to pursue. He says, 'I'd be proud of her if she did anything. I'm glad she's doing something she wants to do.' Nicola later admitted she was scared she would never hit the big time: 'I used to get upset and frightened of it not happening for me, of never getting it and always being a waitress.'

Now, all Nicola could do was wait until that fateful August morning – by the end of the day, she would know whether or not she was in with a chance of being a popstar.

CHAPTER 5

Acting Ambition: Kimberley's Childhood

KIMBERLEY JANE WALSH was born on 20 November 1981 in Bradford, west Yorkshire to parents John and Diane, joining older sister Sally, and later younger siblings Amy and Adam.

Even from a young age, Kimberley was an extremely driven youngster, and attended stage school almost as soon as she could talk. She and sister Sally would provide light entertainment at family gatherings: 'Me and my sister would get up at every family party and do some kind of show for everyone.' She got her first big showbiz break aged five, when she landed a role in ITV kids series *The Book Tower,* which led to her winning the part of Cosette in a production of hit musical *Les Miserables* at the Palace Theatre in Manchester. She explains, 'I've always liked appearing in public. I was at stage schools in Yorkshire from the age of five. From being so young, this is what I wanted to do – this is all I wanted to do.'

She attended Sandy Lane First, then Stoney Lee Middle School in Bradford, juggling her studies with her acting career. She admits even from a young age, her parents were there to cheer her on and encourage her: 'Both mum and dad have been extremely supportive.' she says. 'Mum works full-time as a primary school teacher, so she couldn't be with me at any of the daytime auditions so Dad would take me. But when I was younger she would drive me to stage school every week.'

Her parents dedication to the cause paid off, and Kimberley was offered a role in another ITV series, the hospital-based kids show *Children's Ward*, later renamed *The Ward*. This role got the youngster noticed, and led to many more television roles over the years, including a part in *This Is Personal: The Hunt For The Yorkshire Ripper* (2000), a dramatisation of the investigation into serial killer Peter Sutcliffe's crimes in the 1970s. Her love of drama led to a love of singing, and a young Kimberley dreamed of one day emulating the success of her idol, Kylie Minogue: 'The first record I bought was 'I Should Be So Lucky'. I was a huge fan when I was younger.'

Meanwhile, sister Sally was steadily climbing up the ladder to fame. She landed a part in Yorkshire soap *Emmerdale*, playing student Lyn Hutchinson. Her celebrity status even saw her being asked to switch on the Christmas lights in Derby, but it wasn't long until there would be two Walsh siblings swanning around the world of showbiz. While Kimberley was growing up, there was another addition to the Walsh household: Sally's boyfriend, Bradford City midfielder David Donaldson, who lived with the family from 1999 while the pair were dating. Despite the strain on space in the family's Allerton home, Sally insisted her mum didn't mind having an extra body under her roof. 'It's not exactly a massive house, but we all get on well together,' she said, 'Mum is very understanding.' Stray cat Meg became another addition to the Walsh household around this time. Sally explains, 'We didn't find Meg – she found us. For weeks she kept turning up on our doorstep trying to worm her way into the house and our affections.'

Despite the household harmony, things took a turn for the worse when a 22-year-old model sold her story of a night of passion she shared with David in London while Sally was up in Bradford. Claire Daniels later alleged she was on the receiving end of nuisance calls from a mystery male who was threatening to beat her up. The Walsh family rallied around Sally and devoted sister Kimberley provided a supportive shoulder to lean on.

Keen to gain some financial independence, Kimberley set out to find a part time job in Allerton. She found work in a local bakery, but didn't enjoy the early starts and working for very little money. She says, 'I was a cleaner in a bakery and it was terrible! I used to have to stand inside a freezer to clean it and I worked from 7am to 1pm every Saturday and got paid £10. Then I used to come home and do a big batch of ironing for my mum's friend to make extra cash.'

When she got older, she worked as a waitress at Salts Diner in Saltaire, a purpose-built Victorian model village near Shipley in Bradford. She worked alongside Sally Dawson, a friend of her older sister who would later attempt to emulate Kimberley's popstar prowess on BBC reality talent show *Fame Academy* – despite getting down to the final 26, Sally failed to match her local pal's TV show success. The pair had appeared together years before in a production of the musical *Ellis,* which told the story of Jewish immigrants' new lives in the USA.

In a classic case of what was later to be true life imitating art, a role in BBC education series *Focus 2000* saw Kimberley appear as a singer in an up-and-coming pop group. In another twist, she appeared alongside Kelli Young – a star of the inaugural series of *Popstars* who went on to enjoy chart success with original 'flopstars-done-good' Liberty X. Around the same time, Kimberley was helping out at sister Sally's new drama school, Drama 2000, in November 2000. Aged 21, Sally decided to run drama classes for kids in the Bradford area from a church hall in Allerton. The classes were held on Wednesday evening and Saturday mornings, with Kimberley lending her acting expertise to help coach the actors and actresses of the future. But the school wasn't all about landing parts and nurturing high achievers – Sally wanted her kids to have fun. 'I think a lot of drama schools pressure kids to do well and get the parts,' she said. 'I think it should be more about enjoying yourself and building confidence. Drama lessons can do a lot for children just as an enjoyable hobby. The main thing is it gives you confidence you might not otherwise have.' But Sally was forced to shut the 70-student strong school down to concentrate on her acting career, later landing a part in *Eastenders*.

The dawning of the new millennium brought with it auditions for a starring role in long-running and legendary soap, *Coronation Street*. A new character, hairdresser Maria Sutherland, was to enter the series as apprentice mechanic Tyrone Dobb's girlfriend. It was the break she had been waiting for. But before a Walsh sister legacy was established in soapland, Kimberley eventually lost out to Samia Ghadie after making it to the final four. In another brush with *Popstars* fate, the pre-fame Hear'Say pop pixie Suzanne Shaw was also in the running for the role. After the disappointment of not getting the part, Kimberley vowed to concentrate on her studies and her singing career.

After leaving Beckfoot School, Kimberley enrolled at Trinity and All Saints College in Horsforth, Leeds – a further education establishment accredited by Leeds University – to study English and Media Studies: 'I did the university thing so I wouldn't feel like a complete dosser,' she explains. During her time at university, she appeared in ITV comedy drama *Stan The Man*, which was filmed nearby in Manchester and aired in 2002, just prior to the *Popstars: The Rivals* auditions. She spent two years as an undergraduate student at Trinity and All Saints, but deferred her final year when the *Popstars: The Rivals* auditions were announced. After a childhood spent acting, she knew her real love was singing, and threw herself into the auditions in Manchester with great gusto – would giving up her education at such a late stage pay off?

CHAPTER 6

Popstars: The Rivals

AMID A BARRAGE of egos and self important fame wannabes galore, a new search for the boy and girl bands of the future was launched amid a blaze of publicity, spearheaded by ITV, who would later air the programme documenting the forage for talent in Autumn 2002. Thanks to the success of the ground-breaking Popstars TV talent show format screened across the UK in 2000, thousands of young hopefuls were desperate for their fifteen minutes of fame – and crossed their fingers their time of success would last longer than the show's former winners, Hear'Say.

Hear'Say triumphed during the inaugural series of *Popstars*, beating 'losers' Liberty X in apparent talent and record sales. But the music industry and the public view of manufactured pop acts had changed since the turn of the century. Hear'Say were no longer at the top of their game, and Liberty X had eclipsed them in terms of chart hits and column inches in the tabloid press. Fans had grown tired of the band's manufactured ways, with record sales falling at an alarming rate. Hear'Say finally announced their split in October 2002 – but not before thousands of popstar wannabes had pledged their allegiance to the *Popstars* format in the shape of an application form. Andre Paine, then of music magazine the *NME* said at the time: 'It's over as a phenomenon, it's no longer exciting. *Popstars* and Hear'Say took the magic away.' But despite Paine's death knell, reality TV talent shows were certainly not on the wane – and starlets in the making were lining up to be part of the *Popstars* picture. While the original *Popstars* has-beens had fallen by the wayside, both the winner and runner-up of spin-off show *Pop Idol* were going from strength to strength. Will Young, who emerged victorious on the show, and cute teen Gareth Gates were riding high in the charts and courting musical success – so it was understandable 18–24 year olds up and down the country were extremely keen to emulate the fast-track to fame embodied by the pair.

Details of the new show began to emerge, slowly but surely. This year, the contest would be turned on its head; instead of one mixed group to launch an assault on the chart, five girls and five boys would reignite the age old battle of the sexes, but with a twist – both groups would go head to head in a bid to land the fabled Christmas number one slot. Having the formation of two bands at its core effectively helped distance the show from the failure of Kym Marsh, Noel Sullivan, Suzanne

Shaw, Danny Foster and Myleene Klass in one fell swoop, but the format change wasn't the only shake-up TV bosses planned to employ in order to exorcise the demons of the Hear'Say era.

Popstars executive producer 'Nasty' Nigel Lythgoe announced his decision to step down from the programme's judging panel, after making the decision to leave LWT. Leaving his post as entertainment controller, Lythgoe joined forces with music svengali and infamously sacked Spice Girls manager Simon Fuller at 19 Entertainment to oversee international deals for the *Pop Idol* format. Publicist Nicki Chapman and Paul Adams were also shelved, with a new line-up of judges to cast their critical collective eyes on the UK's emerging new talent. Pop supremo and hit factory helmer Pete Waterman would head up the new judging panel following his success on *Pop Idol* the previous year, alongside Irish music mogul Louis Walsh and former Spice Girl Geri Halliwell.

Louis had been spotted by ITV bosses on the Irish version of *Popstars* earlier that year, and had been their first choice to appear on the programme. But he was keen to mark his territory – and make it known he wasn't just a replacement for the acid-tongued Simon Cowell's nasty persona: 'I'm not the new Simon Cowell. I could be never Simon Cowell. I'm not going to be nasty but I am going to be honest. The reason I was asked to join *Popstar: The Rivals* was because I was part of RTE's *Popstars*. ITV saw me on that programme and I was never nasty on that. They don't expect me to be anything other than myself on this show.' Waterman, famed for making a success of Kylie Minogue, Jason Donovan and Bananarama, would manage the newly formed boy band, while Walsh, who spearheaded the chart dominance of Boyzone and Westlife, would help propel the girl group to pop stardom. Davina McCall would front the series and act as a surrogate mother for the eventually 30-strong brood while away from their families and friends.

Initially earmarked as a 'strictly by invitation only' audition process, show producers had to ditch their closed talent search and open up the path to stardom when thousands of all-singing, all-dancing fame wannabes hounded a *Popstars: The Rivals* hotline after learning they had missed the application deadline. Application forms had been made available from ITV in the summer of 2002, with over 30,000 hopefuls sending in demo recordings showcasing their vocal prowess. Judges whittled down their number to just under 400, with follow-up 'callbacks' held in secret locations in London, Manchester and Glasgow. But due to the overwhelming demand which followed a high-profile launch in August 2002, bosses were forced to hold two additional open auditions at Wembley Conference Centre on 9 August and at the Lowry Hotel in Manchester a week later for those who missed out – with one of these being Sarah Harding, who made her way to the Manchester hotel to sing for her success. And Louis Walsh, on board for the first time, made it clear the new crop of would-be pop stars would have to up their game to impress him – as he didn't think much of previous winners Hear'Say: [Someone like] Myleene may get into the final but she probably wouldn't make it into the group. Nor would the others.'

Luckily for Walsh, he had a secret weapon up his sleeve in the shape of a unfortunate pop starlet from Derry in Northern Ireland. When Nadine Coyle arrived at the Glasgow auditions, Louis was delighted – he knew that with the 17-year-old in his band, they could blow the boys' efforts out of the water. After the debacle surrounding the singer's exit from Irish *Popstars* for being underage, Nadine was undeterred and wowed the panel with her vocal talent. A grinning Walsh told fellow judges Geri and Pete, 'This is my girl, Nadine was in my band in Ireland. I won't let her escape – she's got star quality.' Nadine breezed through to the London stage of the elimination rounds with her performance of Eva Cassidy's 'Fields Of Gold'. But Nadine's Achilles heel was to be her hatred and lack of dancing talent – would her not-so-fancy footwork hold her back in the later stages of the competition? The judges would later describe Nadine's dancing ability as 'wooden'.

A nervous Cheryl Tweedy joined Nadine at the Glasgow audition, although her nerves threatened to eliminate her from the competition before she had even had the chance to sing a note. Cheryl says, 'I used to watch *Pop Idol* but I never thought about going to the auditions. When I turned up at the *Popstars* audition I was going to walk straight back out. I thought I was going to vomit.' Thankfully, the wave of nausea passed and 19-year-old Cheryl impressed the panel with her rendition of S Club's 'Have You Ever'. Choosing a track co-penned by the lady responsible for resurrecting Kylie Minogue's career with 'Can't Get You Out Of My Head', performing a work by pop songwriter and 1990s singer Cathy Dennis was an astute move – as the judges didn't hesitate to put the flowery–top clad teenager through to the next round. Louis admitted almost immediately he wanted to put her through, but wanted to gage just how much the 19-year-old craved a successful singing career. He questioned: 'Do you really want to be a pop singer? Is that all you want to do? You do know it's a really tough life – it's early mornings, late nights and lots of bullshit?', to which a confident Cheryl replied, 'I wouldn't be happy doing anything else.' But it wasn't just Cheryl's voice the panel were amazed by; her good looks helped her win Pete's vote hands down. He told her, 'You have the most beautiful eyes and skin I think I've ever seen in my life,' and later added, 'You'd have to be dead if you didn't think she was stunning. My God!'

At the Manchester auditions, Sarah, Kimberley and Nicola had their chance to unveil their voices. Sarah opted for Steps' 'Last Thing On My Mind', Kimberley chose to perform Whitney Houston's 'Where Do Broken Hearts Go', while Nicola sang Shakira's 'Underneath Your Clothes'. Needless to say, all three had what it took to impress Pete, Geri and Louis, and were on the next train down south to pursue their dreams of becoming popstars.

On 7 September 2002, the hand-picked pop hopefuls would be unveiled to the public when the *Popstars: The*

Rivals show began its 17 week run. The thousands of would-be popstars were whittled down to the 30, and later the final 20 – ten boys and ten girls – but it was to be a tension-fraught final few weeks for the batch of young female singers wanting to be part of a newly formed group. The 20-strong girls and boys were housed in two £2 million luxury mansions in a secret location in Surrey, southern England, where they would live together until their respective numbers were reduced to five apiece, with the girl and boy polling the fewest votes evicted bi-weekly until 10 youngsters were left and the new pop groups formed.

Pete paid a visit to Stockport, where he popped round to Sarah and her mum Maria's home. Unsure of her place in the final ten, she told Pete, 'If I go no further today, I'll say thank you for the experience,' defiantly adding, 'watch this space because I'm not giving up, no way am I giving up.' But it was only good news Pete had to deliver, with a delighted Sarah launching into screams and hugging Pete and mum Maria.

Louis travelled to Nadine's hometown of Derry to break the news. Nadine sat on the sofa with her parents and sister, desperate to hear what her mentor had to say – but knew her lack of dancing skills could be her ultimate downfall. 'I'm really glad you did it,' he said. 'I'm really glad you did it after the Irish *Popstars* fiasco, but we have a problem – Geri Halliwell. She says you cannot dance. You've got the vocals, you've got the looks, you've got the personality... but I've overruled Geri and you're in the final 10!'

The same week, it was the same Geri Halliwell's turn to inform Cheryl it was make or break time up in Newcastle Upon Tyne. Cheryl admitted she hadn't given her all in the past week, and Geri conceded she and the judges had noticed her behaviour: 'So do you want the good news or the bad news? The comments are that we thought that you really held back. We could tell that you did not give your all. As a performer you're beautiful, you absolutely blew us away. You're absolutely stunning looking and there were a lot of people that loved you. Do you feel positive about it?' Cheryl replied, 'I'd like to – not at the minute [though], no.' But Geri couldn't shatter the teenagers dreams: 'Okay so that was the bad news 'cos you're in!' A distraught but elated Cheryl chided the former Spice Girl for her wily ways, saying, 'Geri – you shouldn't do that. That was really horrible. You shouldn't be allowed to do things like that to people.' All was forgotten, however, as it began to sink in she was in with a real chance of pop stardom.

Chloe Staines, Nicola Ward, Emma Beard, Lynsey Brown, Aimee Kearsley, Javine Hylton and Hazel Kanaswarn completed the female finalists line-up, with their male counterparts Daniel Pearce, Jamie Shaw, Andrew Kinlochan, Anton Gordon, Matthew Johnson, Keith Semple, Nikk Mager, Michael Green, Chris Park and Peter Smith battling it out to be their testosterone-heavy rivals.

While the previously 'too young' Nadine went from strength to strength in the competition, another female finalist was feeling the heat of her excess years. Pregnant finalist Hazel Kaneswaran, at 25 years old, was discovered to be 10 days over the age limit by the show's lawyers during the contract signing stage. In a sensational twist, Hazel saw her dreams of stardom dashed when she was axed from the programme at the beginning of October. Louis and Geri flew to Hazel's hometown of Dublin to break the news her 20 June 1977 birthdate broke the show's rules – applicants had to be between 16 and 24 on 1 July 2002.

Kimberley Walsh was drafted in to replace Hazel, after a rollercoaster of emotion. Pete broke the news to the Bradford lass she hadn't made the final 10 girls, but weeks later Louis was able to tell Kimberley that, thanks to Hazel, she was once again in the running for fame. She had kept in touch with finalists Nadine and Cheryl, who she had sent text messages to and had spoken to them both on the phone. But nothing prepared her for Louis' visit. She recalls, 'It was bizarre coming back into the show. I had only just got my head around the fact that I hadn't made the final 10 when Louis Walsh turned up on my doorstep. He pretended he just wanted to do an interview about how I felt about losing out. Then he told me not to audition for anything else as I was back in. I couldn't believe it. I started screaming and crying with joy. My whole family were screaming, "Yes, Yes."'

In another twist of fate for the five girls eventually named Girls Aloud, controversially, finalist Nicola Ward withdrew from the competition in a row over the fine print in the winners' final contract, just a week before the 10 female finalists made their first live studio performances to the viewing public. She said, 'They are trying to make us sign our life away. The contract is outrageous. If we win, we have to sign up to an agreement which means they own us. They can use our faces on mugs or duvets, and God knows what. And we'll only get £1,500 a week for touring while they're raking it in. They'll be making profits from ticket sales, T-shirts and TV interviews and paying us a pittance. It's not worth it. I'm going to concentrate now on getting a solo career and find a company that won't try to control my whole life. Walking away from the show has lifted a huge weight off my shoulders. I'm free again. It was like a prison.'

And Nicola Ward added her predecessors Hear'Say should act as a by-word for talent show failure for the remaining 19 contestants, warning: 'At the end of the day when you look at what's happened to Hear'Say – the last band produced by this programme – I don't think I'm giving up too much.' The girl's group was left in limbo – would another finalist be drafted in to replace the 19-year-old or would the remaining nine battle it out amongst themselves?

None of the remaining contestants expressed such dissent over the contracts, which would see them signed to Polydor records. In 2007, Nicola Ward relaunched her singing career as part of pop duo Cussh, embarking on a UK schools tour – a far cry from what she could have achieved as a member of the final girl group on *Popstars: The Rivals*. But Ms Ward's departure from the competition opened the door for a shy 17-year-old, Nicola Roberts. Nicola made it to the last 15, but was selected to replace her namesake in the girl's £2 million luxury pad in Weybridge, Surrey. Louis said at the time, 'She's very shy and very introverted but she's an amazing singer.' Nicola was brought back onto the show to talk about her experiences on *Popstars,* but was shocked when ITV2's *Popstars* spin-off show host, Another Level's Dane Bowers, broke the news she was back in the running to become a star. She says, 'I just thought I was going to go along to the TV studio to chat about taking part in the show. I could see everybody looking at me and I just wondered what was going on. Then Dane Bowers told me I was going into the house – I was in a state of shock.'

But it wasn't at all plain sailing for the remaining contestants. Something was playing on Sarah Harding's mind – just before the Popstar's auditions, she had sent a saucy picture to lad's mag *FHM* as part of their annual High Street Honey's competition. She said, 'I posted it months ago before I got my big chance on *Popstars: The Rivals*. When I discovered I was actually in the magazine, I panicked. It was the week of my audition and I was terrified. There is nothing I want more than to be a singer and I was up all night worrying myself sick.'

Every other week, the girls would face eviction from their swanky house and their dream of fame. The girls would perform solo, with a second ensemble performance on the show with the other girls. Cheryl, Kimberley and Sarah found themselves in the bottom two on several occasions – despite winning over the judges, they didn't manage to court the public, which was voting in its thousands by phone and text. The night Cheryl came in the bottom two with 16-year-old Aimee, she later admitted she wished she had been voted off in order to save her 'rival'. She said, 'That night I would have preferred to have gone through it so that she didn't have to. She was only young. I was only 19 myself, but I'd taken knocks. I was stronger.' The stress was beginning to get to the girls, who felt the whole process itself was indeed cruel: 'At the back of your mind was that you're constantly working this hard and you don't know what for,' said Nadine, 'You think "I'm doing this, I'm knackered, I've got cold sores, me head's banging, I can't sleep, I'm a nervous wreck and I might get thrown out on Saturday night", so it would all have been for nothing.'

As the girls waved goodbye to their singing pals week after week, 10 soon became six. It was a difficult time for everyone involved, with Nadine forced to leave the house for a few days after a doctor diagnosed her as suffering from stress. It later emerged the singer had found a lump under her arm, sparking fears of a cancerous growth which worried Nadine and her family – and the health scare nearly forced her to withdraw from the competition. Mum Lillian says, 'Until getting the all clear, Nadine thought the worst and feared she'd be out of the race. This was going through her mind when she performed on the show. And she was biting her lip as the judges praised her, secretly fearing she'd have to drop out.'

On 30 November, close friends Nadine Coyle, Sarah Harding, Nicola Roberts, Kimberley Walsh, Cheryl Tweedy and Javine Hylton would lose one of their number – with the remaining five well on their way to becoming household names as part of the UK's newest girl group.

And it wasn't without the support of their respective hometowns. Cheryl's pal John Mulroy masterminded a plan to have a 40 foot long banner decorate local landmark the Tyne bridge – imprinted with the instructions, 'Vote For Cheryl Tweedy, *Popstars: The Rivals*' to passing motorists. John contacted Newcastle City Council prior to the November 30 final, and gained permission to drum up support for Heaton's most famous daughter in the unique way. He said, 'It's great. Geordies support their own – we all want Cheryl to do us proud. I'm sure she will. But it's down to the viewers to make the difference.' But it wasn't just friends and family painstakingly creating banners of support – local newspaper the *Evening Chronicle* produced a 'We're backing Cheryl' banner to help make sure the singer garnered the unequivocal support of the North East.

Nicola's parents made a whole host of 'Vote Nicola' posters and badges in a bid to drum up support for their daughter: and vowed that money was to be no object as they cheered on the Runcorn girl. 'We have been putting posters up everywhere and people have been stopping us in the streets and asking us for badges!' explained mum Debbie. 'We have made about 700 and with all the trips to London we have spent

£1,500 – but money doesn't matter, you do it for your child and find the money from somewhere! Nicola has a fantastic chance of making the band, but the voting can change at the last minute. We want to thank everyone for their support and ask them to get behind the local girl one last time.' Fans in Nicola's hometown were so enamoured of the potential popstar that they were pilfering the posters of support as souvenirs – but luckily the Roberts continued to produce more so their message would be heard. Granddad Gordon revealed, 'The kids have been taking them down for themselves as souvenirs as fast as we can put them up.'

But Nadine's parents worried that the other girls, who lived on the British mainland, would dominate the voting on final night. Dad Niall said, 'Our main fear is that the girls from the big cities in England will get big votes if everyone votes for their own. Hopefully, the support at home will be big for Nadine and hopefully people across Ireland will be able to vote.'

Each took it in turns to perform their songs that evening, knowing that with each minute that passed, they were getting closer to realising their dreams... or losing them forever. A departure from her run of down tempo ballads during the series, Nadine sang Whitney Houston's 'I Wanna Dance With Somebody' to critical acclaim, flanked by Sarah, Javine and Cheryl. Geri lauded the 17-year-old for her choice of a lively number, adding, 'I think it's ironic you picked this song as we all know she doesn't like dancing very much!' Pete branded the performance 'fabulous', while Louis told Davina and millions of TV viewers: 'I think this band is going to be the start of a really really long career for Nadine Coyle. I think she's fantastic and I like her'. Nicola opted for a performance of 'I'm So Excited', Sarah performed a rousing rendition of 'Holding Out For a Hero', while Cheryl stuck to her winning formula of ballads – a genre which had seen her the whole way through her *Popstars: The Rivals* journey.

The girls completed their *Popstars* run with the following:

Cheryl
Week One: Now That I've Found You
Week Two: Still The One – came in the bottom four.
Week Three: Nothing Compares 2U – came in the bottom three
Week Four: Right Here Waiting For You

Nicola:
Week One: River Deep, Mountain High
Week Two: Shout
Week Three: Wind Beneath My Wings
Week Four: I'm So Excited

Sarah
Week One: Build Me Up Buttercup
Week Two: Anyone Who Had A Heart
Week Three: I'll Be There – came in the bottom three
Week Four: Holding Out For A Hero – came in the bottom three

Nadine
Week One: Show Me Heaven
Week Two: Fields Of Gold
Week Three: When I Fall In Love
Week Four: I Wanna Dance With Somebody

Kimberley
Week One: Baby Can I Hold You – came in the bottom three
Week Two: Unbreak My Heart – came among bottom four
Week Three: Emotions
Week Four: Chain Reaction

After their respective performances, the six remaining girls knew all they could do was sit and wait for the verdict. The sextet tentatively waited on the orange *Popstars* sofa – they knew one of them was going home tonight without making the band. Davina exclaimed, 'The countdown to the band starts now... deep breath... it's the girls!' before launching into a montage of their last ever solo performances. Sarah, Nadine and Kimberley sat together in the front sofa, while Nicola, Javine and Cheryl reclined behind them. After a long pause, Cheryl was announced as the first popstrel to be admitted into the *Popstars: The Rivals* hall of fame, voted into the band with a staggering 295,000 votes. Jumping up with her hands in the air, the Geordie made good yelled her battle cry of 'come on' to the millions watching and made her way over to Davina

– the support back home in Newcastle had more than paid off. Cheryl later told the press: 'I couldn't believe it when Davina called me up first. I was just overwhelmed – it was a fantastic feeling and it's still sinking in. I woke up on Sunday morning and I burst into tears because I was just so happy.' And the star thanked her local fans for their support: 'I just want to thank everyone who voted for me, especially everyone from home. People in Newcastle have been so supportive and I wouldn't have made it without their votes. I think the banner over the Tyne bridge must have helped!' But Cheryl admitted the reality of being part of the *Popstars* juggernaut hadn't yet sunk in, and sat on her bed in floods of tears the following morning. 'I was staring and staring at the same spot for over an hour. I couldn't believe it. It was all too overwhelming. I just cried and cried.'

Nicola, Nadine and Kimberley were the second, third, and fourth girl band members respectively, with Sarah and Javine left to face off for the fifth and final spot. Davina called them over from the safety of the sofa to announce to verdict. Sarah hung her head, while Javine closed her eyes and locked Sarah's hand in hers in preparation for the news – and the inevitable; one of the pair would experience one of the biggest disappointments of their lives. Davina called out Sarah's name – much to the singer's surprise. She was visibly shocked, and broke down into uncontrollable tears.

Understandably, the girls' families were elated by their offspring's success and realisation of the quintet's collective childhood dreams. After months of watching their daughters sweat and toil from the sidelines, their hard work and support had finally paid off. Cheryl's mum Joan explains, 'It was brilliant once they announced she was first in the band, but before the show everyone was very tense and worried. I just screamed when she got through – everyone hit the roof. Even after the whole show finished I didn't get to see Cheryl until nearly midnight because she was busy signing autographs. Since we got home yesterday we have had everyone at the door to say congratulations with cards for Cheryl. She has wanted this since she was four years old. She is really happy.'

Despite some of Nicola's acquaintances in Runcorn harbouring negative feelings about her success – people she would later thank for 'spurring her on to succeed' – her family was understandably elated by her success, and cracked open the champagne to toast their eldest daughter's victory after soaking up the experience of the historic night in a London studio. Mum Debbie said, 'The atmosphere was absolutely fantastic. It was really explosive. We all just screamed and were hugging and kissing her. It was mad! We bought her a bottle of champagne for a little toast. I could see the worry had gone from her face, she seemed more relaxed. It has been a rollercoaster for her. She is really excited but you couldn't meet a more down-to-earth girl. She has no airs and graces. Her feet are very firmly on the ground. She thinks it's mad that fans are already waiting to see her. She is going to be an amazing star. The biggest thing will be walking into a record store and seeing her face on the front cover of a CD. It's a lovely feeling for Nicola to have realised her dream.'

Kimberley's family were over the moon by their daughter's success, but were upset at Javine's failure to make the final cut, as she had come to be a good friend of Kimberley's over the show's duration. Dad John said, 'We enjoyed the party afterwards but we were all a little bit upset with Javine not going through. She was close to Kimberley and the rest of the girls. It did put a dampner on the party but after two or three bottles of champagne we started to relax a little bit more!' Mum Diane added they were still coming to terms with the good news: 'It still hasn't sunk in. I think we have been on the edge of our seats from the first show. We've never had one show where we thought we wouldn't be going home. One or two of the other girls have had a comfortable run through.'

Of all the contestants, it was perhaps Nadine who had the smoothest ride on the *Popstars: The Rivals* bandwagon. Nadine took the time to thank everyone from Derry – as she was on the receiving end of unrelenting support from the Irish and Northern Irish contingent who were desperate to see one of their own succeed on the mainland. She said, 'I want to thank everyone at home who has supported me and I can't wait to come to Ireland and perform – that is going to be an amazing moment.'

Sarah's mum Marie, her stepdad Peter, dad John and brother Dave were delighted that she had been voted into a place in Girls Aloud. Sarah's mum explains, 'The whole family is so excited about Sarah making it into the band. We were more nervous than her as the other singers were whittled down. She's such a huge pop fan.' Sarah later admitted her mum was, 'so nervous she nearly had a heart attack!' Thankfully, on the night, she didn't.

But a controversy over phone votes threatened to mar Sarah's success. Uproar abounded from supporters of Javine Hylton who claimed the voting had been incorrectly registered. But an inquest into a flaw in the phone voting system proved the rumours to be unfounded, after viewers claimed they were thanked for voting for Sarah in a recorded message when they had in fact called to register their votes for Javine. A spokesperson for Granada Television confirmed Sarah had received over 50,000 more votes than Javine during the live final, with a spokeswoman for Red Fig – who dealt with the telephone voting system for the show, substantiating Granada's claims: 'The confirmation messages were correct for each number at all times when they were dialled. Throughout the show last night Sarah was ahead of Javine and the text message result mirrored the phone call votes.'

Cheryl, Nicola, Nadine, Kimberley and Sarah could now sleep safe in the knowledge they were Britain's newest pop band, with a record deal with Polydor in the bag, and a life of singing stardom ahead – and that no-one could now take that away from them. But as with all great triumphs, their elation was to be short-lived – they now had five more pressing matters to conquer... Keith

Semple, Matt Johnston, Daniel Pearce, Anton Gordon and Jamie Shaw; the five boys who had been named as One True Voice a week earlier on 23 November.

One True Voice were set to release their interpretation of Bee Gees' classic 'Sacred Trust', with 'Long After You're Gone', a track penned by Pete Waterman and bandmember Daniel as a double A-side. The gauntlet for the Christmas number one was well and truly laid down, when Pete said of the single, 'If this goes in at number two I will commit suicide. I have got to beat Louis Walsh.' But Louis had some ammunition up his sleeve. It had already been announced that one of the songs forming part of the girls' double A-side release would be a cover of East 17's 'Stay Another Day', but the name and genre of the main track was still a mystery. Kimberley was delighted at the choice of 'Stay Another Day' – as a huge East 17 fan in her youth, the song was the first ever single she bought when it was 1994's Christmas number one. Good omens were springing up in the most unexpected places – and at break-neck speed. Nadine explains, 'For me the whole *Popstars* experience was very strange and powerful – you don't have a moment to sit down and think what is actually happening. You are bumped from one stage to the next and every emotion is captured on TV, then you are suddenly thrust out onto the public as winners.'

It wasn't long before details of the new song were uncovered, with the 'feisty and sexy' 'Sound Of The Underground' – a track inexplicably turned down by Louis Walsh's pop protégée Samantha Mumba –

destined to set the UK pop charts alight. It was the start of the girls' symbiotic relationship with songwriting juggernauts Xenomania – little did they know the killer pairing would provide them with a string of chart-busting and critically-credible hits over the next few years. Comparing One True Voice's effort with that of Girls Aloud, it was clear the girls had by far the best debut single – but the girls were unsure of its kick-ass chart-beating prowess. Nadine explains, 'The first time I heard it, I was like, what the fuck is this? It had a drum'n'bass beat, these mad wee surfie guitar bits. It wasn't like a pop record. We had to be taught how to sing like that. Not to leave anything spare.' Kimberley adds, 'I was just glad that it didn't have that mega-cheesy Steps vibe to it. It sounded a bit different. But for a Christmas single? I think we all thought it was fucking crazy.' In the fickle world of pop, however, would teenage girls fall for the sound of their fellow females over the gaggle of gorgeous guys? On 16 December, it was up to the record-buying public to decide who would be victorious in the battle of *Popstars: The Rivals*. Cheryl, Kimberley, Sarah, Nicola and Nadine's faces peered out from five television screens on the cover of their single, pleading with fans to subscribe to a piece of pop history. The girls thought the boys would win, hands down, and so didn't take the battle all too seriously. Kimberley says, 'We thought all the girls would buy their single and we weren't going to get to number one, so we were just having a laugh.'

After making it into the band, Kimberley, Cheryl,

Nicola, Sarah and Nadine had only a few days to film the video for 'Sound Of The Underground', which they did in a disused warehouse. The video saw the girls lined up a row, a microphone apiece, in a metal cage with a drummer and two guitarists. Much dancing and posing with the aid of a microphone stand ensued, with an explosion of glistening tickertape released at the end. But the experience wasn't one the band particularly enjoyed. Nicola explains, 'Making the first video was freezing cold. We started at five in the morning and finished at like three at night in a dark warehouse with no heating.' 'We were filthy,' adds Kimberley, 'Mud all over us – our hands and our clothes.'

The week of the dual releases, things began to get bitchy – but in something of a gender role reversal, it wasn't the girls who were mouthing off about their TV show counterparts... it was the girls who were in the firing line after it was revealed they were ahead of the boys on sales. One True Voice retorted with a series of verbal attacks, saying, 'The girls are trying everything they can to get to number one but they haven't got the talent. The fight is far from over. Even if they have got a slight lead, they've still got a big fight on their hands. The girls can't sing live. They can't harmonise. When they tried to record their single for *SM:TV*, they were so bad they ended up miming.' The band's manager added fuel to the fire when he claimed the girls had not sung on 'Sound Of The Underground', instead alleging the song was recorded by session musicians. Dispelling Pete's nasty claims, it came to light a previous incarnation of the song did exist. 'Sound Of The Underground' had been recorded by defunct British girl band Orchid – whose bandmembers Eve Bicker, Giselle Somerville and Louise Griffiths are credited as backing singers on the single – but was never released, until Girls Aloud and their team heard the song and chose to make it their own. Nadine explained, 'Everybody uses backing vocals – Mariah Carey and Whitney Houston use them and it just makes it sound better. It bulks up and makes it sound better – we're not denying it and we never did.' Bicker also co-wrote 'Love/Hate', which would later appear on the *Sound Of The Underground* album alongside the title track. Cheryl later fired back, 'People heard us singing live on TV for 10 weeks!'

On 22 December, the musical war was won. Girls Aloud had trounced 'vocal harmony group' One True Voice in the charts. 'Sound Of The Underground' went straight in at number one, selling 213,000 copies of the single against 'Sacred Trust's 147,000, which helped it chart at number two. The band was delighted: 'The boys expected it too much,' said Nicola. 'They'd been bigged up so much and then they didn't actually get there.' Girls Aloud now held the record for the shortest time between formation and landing a number one chart position, they were the first band to have a Christmas number one with their debut single, and were the first girl band to debut at number one. After being awarded the 51st UK Christmas number one, 'Sound Of The Underground' held on to the top spot for four weeks before going platinum with sales of 600,000 – clearly displaying Girls Aloud weren't going to fade away as easily as their *Popstars* predecessors.

CHAPTER 7

The First Year

WITH A NO 1 single, two world record titles and a hammering of their male counterparts under their trendy fashionista belts, Girls Aloud were turbo-charged to launch their assault on 2003. But as sure as they had achieved so much in such a short period of time, things began to take a turn for the worse. The girls had been given some well-earned time off over Christmas to spend with their families, and Cheryl, Nicola, Nadine, Sarah and Kimberley were excited about being reunited with their friends and relatives for an uninterrupted fortnight. Kimberley said, 'Since the Popstars final, everything has been so hectic. We'd finish a show or interview, only to be told, "You've only got an hour with them" and then we'd have to leave. Over Christmas we've got two weeks to relax at home without any pressure and I'm planning on enjoying every single second.'

In a cruel twist of fate, the five girls were given some terrible news over their break. On Christmas day, their tour manager and aide John McMahon was tragically killed in a car crash in Stafford. He had been thrown from his Chrysler people carrier when it hit a telegraph pole close to his home. McMahon had been instrumental in orchestrating the girl's chart success with 'Sound Of The Underground', and was a big part of the band's professional life, driving them up and down the country for promotional appearances and interviews. Girls Aloud were devastated by the news of the death of a mentor they had loved and spent every waking hour with, especially at what was such a happy time for the group.

The girls' start to the year was shrouded in tears, when on 7 January, John's funeral took place at St Austin's church in Stafford, Staffordshire. They had cancelled all promotional commitments and appearances for the foreseeable future, as they needed time to cope with their inconsolable grief. Clad demurely in black, Cheryl, Kimberley, Nadine, Sarah and Nicola didn't fight to hold back the tears at the service, which saw them joined by a who's who of the music world to mourn the death. McMahon had worked with Westlife, Boyzone and Craig David before working with Girls Aloud, and was an extremely familiar face on the pop promotions circuit. The 45-minute service saw a tribute performance by Louis Walsh's Irish girls group Bellefire, with the music mogul leading the tributes to the well-loved McMahon. Louis said, 'He was a great guy and the girls and myself are devastated. John was great at his job and respected by everyone in the business. He was a hard worker who got things done.' The funeral procession from the church walked out to the apt words of Tina Turner's 'Simply The Best', which more than summed up the high regard in which McMahon had been held by the British and Irish music industry. Record company Polydor issued a statement conveying the girls' devastation, which read, 'On behalf of the girls and Polydor, we are truly shocked and upset by the tragic loss of someone we all adored and loved.'

The girls would later pay moving tributes to their late tour manager in the sleeve notes of their debut offering *Sound Of The Underground*. Although they had only known him a few weeks, spending almost every waking hour with John had brought the girls extremely close to him and had a huge impact on their lives. Sarah called John 'a father figure and guardian angel', adding, 'You taught us so much in such a short space of time that we were blessed with your presence. Part of you will always live on within Girls Aloud and will always be in our hearts and thoughts'. Kimberley wrote, 'You were an inspiration and we could not have imagined those first few weeks without you.' Cheryl paid her respects to John, while Nicola dedicated their cover of East 17's 1994 Christmas number one to him: 'You're the one who set us off on the right track. 'Stay Another Day' is yours. xx'

After the pain caused by the sudden death of one of Girls Aloud's entourage, the girls threw themselves back into preparations for their new album and forthcoming tour – but the delight of their first performances in front of thousands of fans was soon to be cut short. The 11-date UK tour with rivals One True Voice and other *Popstars: The Rivals* finalists had been slated to begin in March, but was cancelled the month prior due to poor ticket sales. But manager Louis Walsh insisted it was the other billings for the gigs that had deterred the public from attending as Girls Aloud's star quality certainly wasn't on the wane. Instead, he reckoned it was the fault of the tour's co-headliners, Pete Waterman's One True Voice. He said, 'Being associated with One True Voice was not doing them any favours. They were meant to be touring with One True Voice and the others from the programme but it wasn't selling, nobody was buying tickets. Girls Aloud are doing brilliantly and they don't need to be supported by anyone else.' He later added the band would embark on a solo tour at the end of the year, but the plans never came to fruition – Girls Aloud performed their first tour in 2005.

However, the drama and controversy surrounding the band would only get worse. On 12 January, Cheryl was accused of punching a toilet attendant during a night out with Girls Aloud cohort Nicola. Part-time law student Sophie Amogbokpa alleged the Geordie called her a 'fucking black bitch' and launched into a tirade of racial abuse while under the influence of a few too many shandies. Rumours abounded the singer would be sacked from the band, but management and bandmates alike retained a united stance behind the star, supporting her through the subsequent court case and legal battle. It was an extremely tough time for the group, but they vowed to continue with the same gusto that had seen them win *Popstars: The Rivals*.

It didn't help when her brother Andrew and sister Gillian were bound over to keep the peace and fined £100 each by Newcastle magistrates after a series of punch-ups following their star sibling's *Popstars: The Rivals* success. The pair had gone out to celebrate Cheryl's pop career, but began arguing with one another outside the Raby pub in Byker, near their home – after 10 people got involved, a bystander called 999. But the row continued outside Byker Metro station, where they got involved in a punch up with another couple. Andrew suffered a split lip, while another woman was rushed to Newcastle General Hospital after suffering an asthma attack and a black eye.

Not long after, Cheryl's brother Andrew appeared in court over breaking into a stolen car and several glue-sniffing induced incidents in Newcastle. Following Cheryl's arrest and the previous Tweedy scuffles, the tabloids were desperate to know about Andrew's case in minute detail. His lawyer, Lewis Pearson, slammed the press interest in the case, claiming the media was using Andrew's behaviour to give Cheryl a bad name by association. He said, 'He apologises unequivocally for his behaviour. From a boy he has had difficulty with solvent abuse. That is now under control. What upsets him most is the fact that the press are here. [His sister] is a member of a Pop Idols band and they wish to use his conduct to shame her.' Andrew insisted his glue sniffing days were behind him: 'I was going through a bad time. I'm getting myself back on my feet and I've given up the glue.' Cheryl crossed her fingers the intrusive press would soon stop.

It wasn't just the girl from Newcastle who was getting her name in the papers for all the wrong reasons. Sarah Harding's father John told the tabloids he was heartbroken his daughter didn't want to speak to him. 'I would love Sarah to ring me so that we can make a fresh start in 2003,' he said. 'I've left hundreds of messages on Sarah's phone and sent letters and cards over the years, but she has taken her mother's side and refuses to speak to me. I had not contacted Sarah for some months because frankly I'd given up hope. It's tragic because we were so close and there's so much we could be sharing. It's heartbreaking that my only child is refusing to speak to me and won't let me tell her how much I love her.'

'Established' popstars lined up to predict Girls Aloud's demise, with Duncan James of Blue fame casting the first stone – despite he and his bandmates being wowed when they met Cheryl during the filming of the *Popstars: The Rivals* series. Lee Ryan was very taken with the young lady's good looks, yelling unashamedly from off screen, 'You're hot, you're hot', but Duncan – who had clocked up just over one year of fame with Blue since the debut release of 'All Rise' in May 2001 – believed he was well-placed to offer his commentary of Girls Aloud's future; namely that the girls' career would mirror Hear'Say's – short lived. He said, 'With *Popstars: The Rivals*, it'll be just like Hear'Say. Their first single will be their highest-selling song. It will be the peak of their career and if you start at the top the only way to go is down. It'll be exciting for the first six months, but after that, they'll be isolated, insecure and paranoid, not knowing who they can trust.'

The girls were not deterred and ricocheted back into the pop scene again in May. Kimberley was keen to point out the Hear'Say comparison wasn't at all accurate, and that they would treat their predecessors cautionary tale as a learning curve: 'I think we are in a much better position than Hear'Say were. They were thrown straight in at the deep end. We can learn from what happened to them and there is not so much pressure on us either. It is different this time around because the public have chosen us, so at the end of the day, they are the ones who will buy our single.' Earlier in the year, their name had caused a minor upset to ex-All Saints sisters, Nicole and Natalie Appleton, who had planned to call their new album *Aloud*, but changed the name to *Everything's Eventual* in case the name would cause confusion on the shelves.

Laughing in the face of the doom-mongers, the girls spent the first half of 2003 concentrating on recording their debut album, and at last the good news came rolling in. 'Sound Of The Underground' went platinum on 14 March, selling over 600,000 copies, and would later be the 21st best-selling song of 2003. After a gap of almost five months since 'Sound Of The Underground' stormed the charts, the spring of 2003 saw the release of the girls' second single – 'No Good Advice' – and Girls

Aloud knew it was a punky track with attitude. Xenomania had enlisted the help of Lene Nystrom as the track's co-writer. The former Aqua leading lady was no stranger to chart success, with 1997 hit 'Barbie Girl' hitting the chart's top spot and worming its way into the psyche of every man, woman and child in Europe, and the girls' new track was on course to do the same. The band was confident of 'No Good Advice's chart prowess, and were pleased they had been given a punchy punk-rocky-tinged number for their second single, as it proved they weren't insipid one-trick ponies: 'I just don't think we're all into sweet pop, we've got attitude, you know what I mean, and we're not going to hide behind a little cheesy pop song and not bring ourselves out. We're let loose.' explained Nicola. Cheryl had a go at explaining the thinking behind the video, adding, 'We're just five young feisty girls just having fun basically – we don't need no good advice, we don't need any bad press, we're just having a laugh.' It was this 'attitude' that the producers of the 'No Good Advice' video were keen to harness, and masterminded an edgy storyline accordingly. After the perils of the warehouse-shot visual accompaniment to 'Sound Of The Underground', the band was overjoyed by the news the shoot would take place in a studio. Dressed to the high heavens in space-age silver garments, the girls cavorted from 5am until late into the night against a simple black backdrop punctuated by shimmering lights, a beaten-up pink convertible and a beaten-up phone booth. Sarah had the enviable task of shoving a phone handset through a glass panel to demonstrate just how hard Girls Aloud were – One True Voice were no doubt quaking in their designer trainers. As well as cavorting in and around the pink vehicle in the name of art, the girls were given just three days to learn their tambourine shaking dance, but managed to pull the routine off successfully without the featured percussion stealing the show. Despite later admitting they didn't enjoy the experience, the girls channelled their inner rock chicks and danced to their hearts content. But the list of mishaps was endless. Cheryl cried because her shoes were too tight, deeming the shoot as 'such an awful day' and Sarah had an unfortunate accident with her outfit. She says, 'It was an experience we learned from. So much went wrong in that video. It was a 24 hour shoot. My trousers ripped in the worst place. I just think we've moved on so much that to look back, right the way back to then, it's like "What were we doing?"' The song was finally released on 12 May, and sold 42,762 copies in its first week, taking it to number two in the charts – the group were unable to shift R Kelly's 'Ignition' from the top spot.

The following week, Girls Aloud's first foray into the world of the long player was unleashed. *Sound Of The Underground* was a 15-track showcase of the girls' singing talents, proving they could out-pop many of their contemporaries including One True Voice, who were yet to release a second single, never mind an album. Pop music's big hitters had lined up to co-write and produce the band's songs, with a star-studded line-up of chart favourites and musical stalwarts adding fuel to Brian

Higgins and Xenomania's songwriting fire. Heading up the list was pop veteran Alison Clarkson, who rose to fame as Betty Boo in the late Eighties, threw her weight behind the girls, penning the quirky dance-tinged 'Mars Attack', 'Boogie Down Love' and 'Love Bomb', and producing the songs with The Beatmasters. B*Witched star Edele Lynch co-wrote 'Some Kind of Miracle', with 'Love/Hate' penned by Orchid bandmembers Niara Scarlett and Eve Bicker. Swedish hitmaking supremos Anders Bagge and Arnthor Birgisson, who had enjoyed success writing for Madonna, Take That and Nick Lachey's boy band 98 Degrees were also brought on board. Though perhaps the most high profile collaborator was Westlife's Brian McFadden, who surprised many with an uptempo number, the punningly titled 'Girls Allowed' – it was a far cry from the slushy ballad driven numbers favoured by Louis Walsh's other famous five-piece. Louis sung his liege's praises from the rooftops and his cries were picked up by the British tabloids, 'Brian's been in the studio writing and recording with them all week. I've listened to everything they've come up with. Everyone's favourite track is called 'Girls Allowed'. It's an uptempo number which I'd best describe as sounding like an early Spice Girls track.'

Girls Aloud's relationship with Xenomania would prove to be the making of the group. Brian Higgins was well-versed in what pop pickers' ears longed for – no-nonsense tunes with a killer hook. He was the man responsible for Cher's breakthrough vocoder-assisted number one 'Believe', which topped the charts in the

UK for a spectacular seven weeks, and Dannii Minogue's saucy dance-romp 'All I Wanna Do'. The girls were taken under the wing of the Xenomania production house, and gave a sassy delivery to the tunes and lyrics penned by Brian, singer Miranda Cooper et al. It was the beginning of a beautiful relationship. Girls Aloud's string of sure-fire pop successes were masterminded by Xenomania, and modestly, the group recognised the company was crucial to their popularity – but knew theirs was a symbiotic pairing. Speaking after the release of second album *What Will The Neighbours Say?*, Cheryl said, 'It would be a shame if someone like our producer Brian Higgins went unnoticed. He can't sing a note and he definitely couldn't front 'Love Machine' or 'Biology'. Those songs would never have come to light if it hadn't been for us. We do our best in the studio, and our best to sell the song to the audience when we're out there, but the production of the songs, and how good and fresh they sound, that's all down to the brilliant hard work of Brian and all the people at Xenomania. Without [Xenomania] there wouldn't be any us. I truly believe [they] are the best at what they do.'

'It infuriates Brian when people say bad things about us not writing our own songs,' added Kimberley. 'He's like, I couldn't have this kind of success without you and the whole team of people around us. The way we look, the way we are as people – all of that inspires Brian to write. We just sing bits and pieces of the songs and he builds the music around us. Our vocal performances are a big part of the song, though.' Supremo Brian is equally as complementary about his young charges, especially Nadine, whose talent he reckons is hugely underrated – but he is certainly not alone in his belief she is 'one of the finest singers this country has produced, but I've never seen her referred to as such'.

The weight of the Xenomania and friends' songwriting clout wasn't enough to propel them to number one. The album charted at a highly respectable number two, just behind Justin Timberlake's debut *Justified*. But the critics were convinced of the album's greatness, branding it 'the best pop record you will hear this year'. Paul Connolly of *The Times* wrote, 'It may possess one of the most misleading album titles coined (unless you are someone who thinks Cliff Richard is a little raucous), but this debut from Girls Aloud is one of the best pop records that you will hear all year. This album is packed with so many hit singles that by the end of the summer you will wish you had never heard of Girls Aloud. Tracks such as 'Some Kind of Miracle' (which drew comparisons to Madonna's 'Beautiful Stranger'), the glam stomper 'No Good Advice' and the squelchy disco of 'Mars Attack' are songs that are begging to be loved. *Sound of the Underground* is prepackaged, cynical pop music – but with tunes this great, who cares?'

The girls celebrated with a gig at London's G-A-Y, treating fans to a taster of the album and the two singles they had released so far as part of the six-song set. Revellers sang along and boogied to 'Sound Of The Underground' and 'No Good Advice' while the girls danced on stage clad in customized school uniforms – very much working the cool girl in the form above who got away with wearing non-regulation schoolwear look. Nicola's miniskirt featured the mantra 'I am a rude ginger bitch... botherd [sic],' artfully painted on by Nadine. But the girls weren't too bothered about the spelling inaccuracy, claiming it was a dig a Busted's Matt Willis, who had called Nicola 'a rude ginger bitch' earlier in the year because she allegedly blanked him. Nicola retorted that Matt was merely 'a sad little boy'.

Despite their debut offering missing the top spot, Louis was still confident his brood of beautiful and talented girls would continue to dominate and reinvent the pop world. He had dubbed them 'the Spice Girls with personalities' – much to the annoyance of a visibly irked Melanie 'Sporty Spice' Chisholm, – one fifth of perhaps the most prolific girl band of all time. She told Louis, 'Well, when they rack up 37 million albums worldwide, come back and talk to me.' But her remarks only made the Irishman more determined to better the Spice Girls' success. And he knew Girls Aloud were the only ones on the current music scene who could ever come close. The Spice Girls made their millions in the late 1990s from chart-topping releases, movie deals and a product endorsement list longer than the average arm. Ironically, around the same time as Louis' brush with girl-power megabucks muscle, the British press alleged that Girls Aloud were earning a paltry £80 per day. The *Sun* reported the girls were suffering from spiralling debt problems thanks to their low earnings, with what they did earn being poured back into record label Polydor to cover the cost of recording two singles, and album and a plethora of promotional photo and video shoots. But the record company knew any money spent on promoting Girls Aloud was a sound investment – as the girls were talented enough to recoup the costs. On 6 June, much to the band's delight, the *Sound Of The Underground* album went gold, with over 100,000 copies sold.

On the back of their chart success, Kimberley and Nadine decided to invest in an apartment together in a complex in north London. The pair were ready-made flatmates after their time spent sharing a room in the *Popstars* house, and admitted they loved their new plush girly pad – with the rest of their bandmates living in the same complex or nearby. Nadine said, 'Buying with Kimberley was a natural progression from the time we spent in the *Popstars* house. Kimberley and I shared a room in the house and Cheryl and Nicola were sharing too, while after her roommate was voted off, Sarah was by herself. So when it came to buying apartments it was a natural progression from that really. When we're at home we light our wee candles and have the place looking really romantic – even though it's just me and Kimberly sitting there, looking round and every now and again saying to each other: "Isn't this lovely? This is ours, you know!"'

In August 2003, the girls' gender battle was finally over. Their *Popstars: The Rivals* foes announced that after nine months and two singles together, they were splitting up, following the departure of Daniel Pearce in June. The shockingly corny and embarrassing-titled 'Shakespeare's Way With Words', which, despite being co-written by Eighties pop wunderkind Rick Astley, had only managed to chart at number 10 in June. Members of the band's young fan base felt alienated by the boys highfalutin' reference to the Bard. One fan wrote on Amazon.co.uk, 'After following the boys thru the TV series and loving sacred trust (I'm now just over it not getting to no. 1) I was really disappointed with this single. I hope their next single isn't about Shakespeare. If it isn't I think it will go to no. 1.' The girls, however, were sympathetic over the band's demise; after all, they had both been borne from the same stable and knew each other as friends. After the split, Sarah said, 'They are all talented boys who worked as hard as us and deserved to do well out of it. They just had the wrong songs. For whatever reason, they did not gel as a group in the same way as we have.'

Stoical as ever, Girls Aloud took One True Voice's demise in their stride and once again hit the charts with another top single. 'Life Got Cold' was the group's first ballad, but the slow pace was a hit with new fans – the 18 August release helped bolster the sales of the debut album. 'All of our songs have been uptempo and quite dancey,' explained Cheryl. 'We just wanted a really beautiful ballad that shows off all our voices, and just to show a variety; that we can actually sing a slow song – and that we can actually sing.' After a string of promotional appearances and interviews, the song charted at number three – giving the band a 1-2-3 run with their first three singles. The accompanying video was also something of a departure from its highly polished and high octane predecessors. The girls once again hooked up with director Phil Griffin, who had helmed 'Sound Of The Underground' in December; Phil would later direct music videos for Victoria Beckham, McFly and Amy Winehouse. This time, to match the slow haunting melody, Kimberley, Nadine, Sarah, Nicola and Cheryl were filmed in slow motion looking ponderous and moody, debuting their serious faces for the screen. Almost unbelievably, it was filmed in a studio in east London, despite its convincing alfresco 'abandoned New York City' look.

Meanwhile, Nadine was busy rubbing shoulders with the glitterati in August – the worlds of Irish pop and politics had collided for Westlife star Nicky Byrne's wedding to the daughter of Irish Prime Minister Bertie Ahern. Nicky and his fiancée Georgia Ahern wed in a quick ceremony in Wicklow just days before heading to France for a marital knees-up. Nadine's services had been enlisted by the couple to perform at the lavish nuptials at a reception at Chateau D'Esclimont, one of the country's most exclusive getaways. An Irish pub was constructed to make the guests feel right at home, while the caterers flew in food from Ireland for the pair's special day. Rounding off the Gaelic theme was Nadine, who flew in especially to sing Celine Dion's 'Because You Loved Me' for the couple and guests. And in true pop legacy tradition, the wedding would not have been complete without Louis Walsh's golden boy and former Westlife manager making an appearance. Ubiquitous

Irish crooner and founding member of pops old guard, Ronan Keating, performed 'I Love The Way You Love Me' – one of his previous hits with his former band Boyzone. Nadine brought bandmate Kimberley as her guest to the wedding to support her at the high-profile event. 'I was only too happy to go along with Nad to give her a bit of moral support,' says Kimberley. 'She was singing at the service and was a bit nervous as it was a very big event. It was a beautiful wedding. And I was really proud of her.'

The girls got their first taste of movie soundtrack stardom in September when it was announced they would provide the lead track for new Brit romantic flick *Love Actually* – the directorial debut of revered *Four Weddings and A Funeral* (1994) and *Notting Hill* (1999) writer Richard Curtis. Girls Aloud would record a new version of the Pointer Sisters 1984 hit 'Jump', delving into the world of releasing cover versions for the first time to the tune of a rumoured £500,000. In the movie, Hugh Grant would star as the Prime Minister, while ex-*Eastenders* actress Martine McCutcheon would play a tea lady in 10 Downing Street – which would later be the setting for the accompanying video. The girls frolicked around the nearest thing to the seat of British ministerial power as was possible – a mock up of the Prime Minister's residence transposed to Addington Palace in Gravel Hill, Croydon. Nadine, Sarah, Kimberley, Nicola and Cheryl creep in through a window to the wood-veneered walls of power before running amok in their high fashion combo of smart casual sportswear – teamed with high heels, naturally. The footage of the girls is interspersed with that of the film, resulting in a 'Girls Aloud spy on the Prime Minister' scenario. The girls would later dabble in politics with an interview with high-brow magazine *New Statesman* in 2006, but for now, they were content to stay on the periphery of politics and just have fun.

Fun and celebration was to abound in early October when the band's youngest member, Nicola, reached the milestone of her 18th birthday. Her parents threw a surprise party in Runcorn, with 400 well-wishers – including friends, relatives and former teachers. Nicola was dying to find out what had been arranged, but her parents pulled out all the stops for her coming of age at local club the Bank Chambers. 'We blindfolded her,' said her dad, Paul. 'She tried to guess where we were going but we took her on a detour. It was absolutely superb. She spent two hours meeting and greeting everyone.'

Later that month, the girls took part in a TV special for ITV – a star-studded musical extravaganza celebrating the wonder of *Grease* – imaginatively titled *Greasemania*. Girls Aloud performed 'Hopelessly Devoted To You', while other pop acts such as Darius and Lisa Scott-Lee belted out other numbers from the 1978 John Travolta-Olivia Newton-John smash on the Amanda Holden-fronted show. It was a dream come true for Kimberley, whose favourite movie was the Rydell High-set classic: 'It is always a close thing between *Pretty Woman, Dirty Dancing* and *Grease* [for her favourite film]. If they do make *Grease 3* I'd love to be one of the

After Girls Aloud won *Popstars: The Rivals*, they reached the Christmas 2002 number one spot in an unprecedented three weeks, with over 600,000 sales of 'Sound of the Underground'. Here (*above*) they are pictured at one of their early performances at London's Hammersmith Palais.

Below: At the end of their first summer together, Nicola, Sarah, Nadine, Kimberley and Cheryl pose outside the Royal Albert Hall.

Bradford girl Kimberley Walsh attended stage school from the age of five and never stopped aiming for success until her ambition to be a performer was realised. Here she is pictured on a night out with her sister in Leeds *(above)*, and performing at a concert in Hull *(right)*.

Nicola is the youngest member of Girls Aloud. When her parents organised a lavish surprise 18th-birthday party for their daughter, it took two hours for her to meet all the guests!

Cheryl was announced as the first member of the *Popstars: The Rivals*-formed group, winning almost 300,000 votes from an adoring public.

Sarah comes from a musical family, and has her dad to thank for her first session in a studio – aged just three.

Nadine was devastated when she was axed from Irish *Popstars* band Six for being too young, and thought her chances of fame and fortune were shattered When she arrived at the *Popstars: The Rivals* audition in Glasgow, pop mogul Louis Walsh was delighted.

Above: Girls Aloud have had huge success throughout Europe, with number ones in Greece and Ireland. They are pictured performing in Rotterdam, Holland, in 2005.

The girls know how to party after a demanding show – *(left)* Cheryl photographed as she leaves a London bar, and *(right)* Sarah making a stylish entrance to a private members club.

They're stylish and they've got attitude… and they've also had a record-breaking fifteen top-ten singles and been named the most successful reality TV group ever by Guinness World Records.

Pink Ladies – my perfect role!' They took to the stage once again at the National Music Awards at the Carling Hammersmith Apollo in London in October, but came away empty handed. Still, safe in the knowledge they had more musical surprises up their sleeves for the year ahead, Girls Aloud weren't too disheartened by their lack of trophies.

Tabloid reports in October claimed promotion for 'Jump' was hit with a forced delay due to Cheryl's assault case being heard in Kingston Crown Court in October, and that PR bosses had been unhappy with the singer's negative press enveloping Girls Aloud's *Love Actually* tie in, but the song was finally released on 17 November, when it hit number two – the group's fourth top five single. A well-publicised Battle of The Louis Walsh-managed acts saw Westlife's cover of Barry Manilow's 'Mandy' take the top spot. A week later, on 30 November, Girls Aloud dropped to the number six spot in a reality TV-dominated top ten, starring Will Young's 'Leave Right Now' at number one, and Gareth Gates' 'Say It Isn't So' three places lower. It looked like *Popstars* and *Pop Idol*-generated successes were here to stay. At the end of the month, Girls Aloud saw their debut album go platinum, with sales in excess of 300,000.

A re-issue of the *Sound Of The Underground* album was released on 1 December 2003, with a new cover shoot, the original running order rejigged and the addition of Jump. Two new songs made it onto the album, including a cover of Duran Duran's 'Girls On Film' and coincidentally, another film soundtrack song –

'You Freak Me Out'. The song had been recorded for the remake of classic 1970s Jodie Foster-as-a-teenager role-reversal body swap movie *Freaky Friday*, this time starring Lindsay Lohan and Jamie Lee Curtis as her mother. The girls were pleased with the punchy track, and delighted they had been asked to record it for the film: 'It's a great track and the film is fantastic,' said Nadine, 'We're really honoured to have been asked to do it.'

Besides the group's brush with films, some of the band turned their attention to modelling. Nicola and Cheryl hit the catwalk in November for charity at Liverpool's Newz bar. Cheryl, clad in a pink top/short skirt combo and Nicola, in a white smock and trousers showed their support for the city's Lily Centre, a breast cancer support group. It was a cause close to Cheryl's heart, as she tragically lost her grandmother to the disease. She explains, 'My nan died of cancer at the age of 57. She had lung cancer which then spread, so I am always keen to support any kind of cancer charity. It was really important to me to do this fashion show. I think the Lily Centre does fantastic work, offering help and support to women when they are at their very lowest point.'

The close of the year proved to be a busy time for the band, with their social calendars filled to the brim before their Christmas break. They performed on the last ever episode of Saturday morning's hangover TV favourite *SM:TV* with fellow reality TV singers Gareth Gates and Liberty X; brought their mums to the UK premiere of *Freaky Friday*; visited the children's ward at Sutton's Royal Marsden Hospital, chatting and signing autographs before being interviewed on hospital radio. Sarah even found time to squeeze in a one-day visit to Lapland to see Santa with boyfriend Mikey Green, of *Popstars: The Rivals* losers Phixx. Rumours of a Girls Aloud-starring horror movie abounded, and was slated to begin filming in March 2004, but nothing ever came of the girls' alleged big screen plans. Speaking in July 2004, Sarah said, 'We said we'd like to do a horror film, but that was just speculation.'

The rest of December saw Girls Aloud taking to the stage at TV music show *Popworld's Christmas in Popworld*. Despite a well-documented hatred of hosts Simon Amstell and Miquita Oliver – Nicola once referred to Amstell as 'a right horrible bitchy old queen that needs his hair cutting' – the group shared the bill with Emma Bunton, Busted, Liberty X and Westlife. Dorian Lynskey, music critic for the *Guardian*, deemed Girls Aloud's performance 'a shambles' but conceded that 'Sound Of The Underground's breakbeat stampede is still the best thing to emerge from reality TV.'

The festive season meant holiday time for Nicola, Nadine, Sarah, Kimberley and Nadine. The Derry girl couldn't wait to get back home to Northern Ireland, and even planned to do a spot of karaoke in her mum and dad's bar. She said, 'As soon as work is over we're out necking cocktails and having a really good laugh. But over the Christmas holidays I'll be having a break to spend time in my mum's bar. My dad has got some karaoke equipment so we'll all have a sing-song – just for a change.'

After a short break with their families back home, Girls Aloud rounded off their year by performing for their legions of gay fans by returning to London's infamous G-A-Y club. The venue, along with the booking talents of promoter Jeremy Joseph, has an unequalled reputation for bringing the best acts in the pop world to the Astoria. On New Year's Eve, the girls raided the Christmas fairy's dressing-up box and strutted their stuff in red satin puffy frocks, complete with angel wings. Nicola and Cheryl welcomed in the New Year with a kiss, which was reported as a lesbian clinch by the tabloids à la Britney and Madonna's steamy same-sex smooch at the MTV Music Awards earlier that year. 'It was a New Year's kiss, that's all,' insisted Cheryl.

Girls Aloud had done themselves proud in 2003, and shocked many critics in the process with the quality of their music and complete deference to the god of pop. They had reinvented the 'manufactured band' mould, and the charts and the media were their oyster – despite the negative drawn-out press which had plagued Cheryl's assault back at the beginning of January.

CHAPTER 8

Cheryl in the Dock

DRESSED UP FOR an evening on the tiles, the farthest thing from Cheryl Tweedy's mind was spending a night in the cells thanks to an 'incident' in the early hours of a chilly January 2003 morning. What began as an innocuous New Year night out for Cheryl and fellow Girls Aloud star – Nicola Roberts turned out to be the start of a long-running nightmare for the feisty Newcastle girl. The events that were to unfold at a bar in southern England that evening would overshadow Cheryl's singing career for years to come. The incident, which was initially reported as a 'minor scuffle' by the press, was to prove a trying time for the diminutive Miss Tweedy.

Arriving at The Drink nightclub in Guildford, Surrey, on Friday 10 January 2003, the newly-anointed pop pair were looking forward to a celebration of the past year's hard work and chart success – winning a place in Girls Aloud after an arduous televised journey, and landing a coveted Christmas number one – toasting what was to be a record-breaking year ahead. Cheryl and best pal Nicola had called into the club after a lengthy 12-hour stint recording at a local studio, and planned to spend the night winding down. All appeared to be going to plan, with autograph hunters and fans chatting to the famous chart-toppers over a few glasses of wine and flutes of champagne at the bar. But things went awry when a drunken Cheryl headed to the lavatory and found herself in a lot of trouble over a lollipop at 1am.

Toilet attendant and part-time law student Sophie Amogbokpa, 39, would later claim in court: 'The slim one, Nicola, came out of the cubicle first. She used some of the things put out, like cosmetics – and took some blusher and a bit of make-up. When the fatter, shorter one Cheryl Tweedy came out, Nicola asked her to pay. But she said she wouldn't give me any money and she started picking things up herself. She took some lollies and some chewing gum and a bottle of perfume.' According to Sophie, Cheryl launched a tirade of verbal abuse on her while a frightened Nicola attempted to restrain her bandmate, but the star allegedly punched the attendant in the face, and was later claimed to have called her racist names with the brawling ladies pulled apart by the club's bouncers. Cheryl was arrested and whisked away to a cell with police – where she would spend the next 10 hours before being released on bail the next morning – while Sophie was taken to the Royal Surrey County Hospital for treatment to her black eye. After the incident, toilet mistress Sophie told the press,

'I was shocked. I don't care how many number ones she has had, if she was nobody she shouldn't have said those things to me or hit me. I had done nothing to her and whoever gives me an eye like this should be punished.' Cheryl later described her time in police custody as frightening: 'It was scary. I mean I'd never been arrested before or anything like that. It was cold, it smelt funny, it was just an awful experience.'

But the case wasn't as clear cut as it seemed – a punch thrown at Cheryl had found its way to her cheek during the scuffle. A planned 11 February appearance on *Ant and Dec's Saturday Night Takeaway* had to go ahead, despite the furore caused by the incident – and despite Cheryl's black eye. Resourceful makeup artist Christopher Ardoff, working on the ITV show,was forced to be creative with the Geordie singer's bruised face, hiding the star's battle scars under a heavy layer of foundation and cover-up. But it wasn't Cheryl's scuffle Sophie and the press chose to focus on – it was the alleged racist slur Cheryl had made towards the toilet attendant during the fight.

Unsurprisingly, it wasn't just Cheryl who was devastated by the allegations. Mum Joan was in a state of shock when she received a phone call from Cheryl the morning she was bailed by police, but knew her daughter wasn't a candidate for racial abuse – and made sure the public knew the truth. She said, 'Cheryl is a quiet, sensitive girl who has never been in any trouble. I can't imagine she started the fight. She is absolutely devastated at newspaper reports of what she is supposed to have said to this woman. I am trying to calm her down because she has been on the phone in tears.'

Joan was keen to point out her daughter wasn't a racist; painstakingly listing Cheryl's pro-black credentials. Cheryl had a history of being a fan of black singers, and had dated former child star Hadyn Eshun, frontman of 1990s pop group Ultimate Kaos. The star was also best friends with Javine Hylton and former boyfriend Jacob Thompson – both fellow contestants on *Popstars: The Rivals*. Joan explained, 'She grew up loving music made by coloured artists and Javine was one of her closest friends on the *Popstars* show. Cheryl has been speaking to Javine this weekend and she has given her her full support.' Cheryl's cousin Andrea Bell, married to Caribbean-born Jeffrey Blaize, also stepped in, taking the opportunity to defend her now infamous relative: 'Cheryl was round here at Christmas. She's certainly not a racist and it is terrible she has been branded that. She doesn't distinguish between people for the colour of their skin. She is a lovely girl with a lovely, gentle nature. She has coped really well and her mum has been a big support, although I know it has been hard on them both. I think we are all hoping this can be forgotten about. I am surprised at the amount of attention it has received; I think Cheryl is just looking forward to getting on with her career and putting this behind her.' Record company Polydor hurriedly issued a statement. 'Cheryl obviously deeply regretting getting into the fight,' they said, 'but when the terminology that she was supposed to have used came out yesterday, she was shocked and absolutely distraught.' In one fell swoop, it looked like Britain's brightest pop starlets had burned out before they'd even had the chance to fulfil their chart-beating potential.

Getting thrown out of a nightclub in her hometown just a few weeks later did little to alter the public's perception of the singer as a boisterous party girl. Cheryl had organised a 'girls night out' to the Baja Beach Club in Gateshead, not far from the star's family home. A night on the tiles with her mum was far from a rare occurrence for Cheryl, as her mum is her best pal: 'My mum is more like a friend. I can talk to her about anything; boyfriends, sex, and we go out together a lot to clubs. We get dressed up and have a right laugh.' With mum and self-appointed guardian Joan in tow, the then 19-year-old was asked to leave after being accused of starting a water pistol fight with a group of Newcastle United footballers, also out on the razz for the weekend. Again, it was Joan who stood up for her daughter, dismissing the reports Cheryl was once again drunkenly misbehaving: 'Cheryl loves to dance and we went to Baja to do just that. There was a bunch of Newcastle players there and they came over to talk to her. She was just standing with them. Some of them were playing with water pistols, but not Cheryl. I saw it all happen and I was horrified. I went out with Cheryl to make sure nothing happened to her. The bloke who asked her to leave looked in a real strop. We were all there just to have a good time, minding our own business. I don't know what the problem was.'

Cheryl appeared before magistrates in Guildford on 25 March accused of racially aggravated assault, and was remanded on bail until a hearing later on that year – tabloid reports at the time highlighted the maximum penalty for such an offence, suggesting the star could be jailed for up to two years. In a show of solidarity with their maligned bandmate, the remaining four Girls Aloud-ers made their views on the scenario known, telling the public they would support Cheryl, despite reports to the contrary. The British tabloids had a field day surmising over the band's future, insisting record company Polydor would oust the outspoken Geordie from the Girls Aloud line-up, spelling the end for UK pop's brightest stars. Supportive Sarah said, 'We've made a pact to stand by Cheryl, regardless of what happens. We all love her and know her well. We have pulled together and support each other so much that stuff like her court case isn't going to come between us.' Nadine would later support Sarah's sentiments, insisting Cheryl's position in the band was never an issue with the other members of Girls Aloud. She said, 'We never once considered that we were going to throw Cheryl out of the band, and no-one else could make that decision. We're really strong in our belief that no-one can take it away from us except ourselves. It was really hard for Cheryl because it had gone on so long. But all you can do is be there and support her and hopefully things will go for the best.'

With her bandmates well and truly behind her, on 4 June 2003, Cheryl appeared before Guildford

Magistrates Court in Surrey at a five minute hearing, during which she spoke only to confirm her name, age and address. The case was adjourned until a further hearing at Kingston Crown Court, with the singer given conditional bail. A difficult period ensued for Cheryl, who could only wait for her case to be heard. Her fate was in the jury's hands, and on 9 October, Cheryl's trial was to begin. The week before, her mum moved down to her London home to offer her support. 'I just wanted her there with me – I couldn't have coped without her. She was my rock,' conceded Cheryl.

Appearing at Kingston Crown Court in a white suit, Cheryl denied the charges of racially aggravated assault and occasioning actual bodily harm. Toilet attendant Sophie relived the alleged attack nine months earlier, telling the court of her ordeal in The Drink's lavatories with Cheryl and Nicola. She explained, 'Nicola was trying to restrain her [Cheryl] and looked frightened at how abusive she was. Phil [White, the club's manager] came in and he is a very big bloke. But she was still coming at me. She got close to me and punched me in the left eye. I can't remember which hand she hit me with but she hit my glasses and my glasses fell down. I was taken off to the staff room. An ambulance was called to take me to the hospital.'

Six days into the trial, it was a tearful Cheryl's turn to appear in the dock – and she told the jurors she had acted in self-defence. She took the witness box on 15 October to give her version of events. She explained, 'I came out of the toilets and Nicola said she wanted some lollipops. I walked over to the lollipops and said to the toilet attendant, "I'll take five of these". It became apparent there was a problem. I don't remember what she was saying – she was gesturing with her hands, ranting and raving. At first I thought it was the amount I was taking, but I intended to pay for them. I thought they would be about 20p each, like in any normal shop.

'I said, "Hang on a minute and I will get the change out of my bag." I rested my bag on the sink so I could get my change and I could see her leave her chair and approach me. I think she thought I was just going to take them without paying. The next thing I felt was a blow to my face, on my cheek. I remember grabbing the right side of my face in shock. I was stunned. I wasn't expecting it. I was scared and angry. I remember saying, "What the f**k are you doing?" and I shouted at Nicola to get the management. I was swearing at the toilet attendant, but I didn't call her "a f**king black bitch". We were both shouting and I was thinking, "How the hell do I get out of this one?" She's a big woman and scary-looking, with broad shoulders. I was scared of what she was going to do. I whacked her back, but I don't know how hard I hit her. There's no way I'm going to stand there and let someone hit me when I can defend myself.' And Cheryl added the incident hampered the next day's TV appearance on Ant and Dec: 'As I went to get the [money] out of my bag, I felt this whack on my face. I thought, "My God, the last thing I need is a mark on my face, I have to do a live TV show today." I was angry and scared and upset. I had a swollen cheekbone. I was frightened. What happened if she kept hitting me and blackened my eye and I have got a show tonight?' Cheryl admitted she yelled at Sophie, but denied she had made racist comments at any time, 'There's no way, no matter what state I am in, I would refer to anybody by their colour. I know in my heart, Sophie Amogbokpa knows in her heart and the Lord above knows the truth of what happened, and that's all that matters to me.'

Acid-tongued prosecutor Patricia Lees branded Cheryl 'full of her own self-importance' during the tense high profile trial. She told the Kingston courtroom, 'Here was this woman telling her – the girl who had been to the VIP suite, given champagne – to pay for lollipops. How do you think she took it? Who was behaving well or badly? The sober lavatory attendant who might lose her job, or the drunk Cheryl Tweedy?', and argued an inebriated Cheryl 'staggered out' of the toilet cubicle before a 'verbal exchange' between the pair began. She claimed Nicola then left the toilet, at which point manager White entered the fray: 'I saw Cheryl Tweedy right hook the attendant,' he told the court. 'I picked up Miss Tweedy so she couldn't cause any further damage to the attendant but she was very aggressive and abusive. She was saying, "Get that f**king black bitch up here and I will finish the job. You get that jigaboo up here and I will sort her out."'

It was a trying time for Nicola, who had seen the brawl first hand, and was called to the witness stand, where she confirmed her pal was acting in self defence. She said, 'I told Cheryl to give some change to the attendant. But as she got the change out the lady just punched her in the face. Cheryl told me to get the management and I ran to the security guard. He ran in and I saw the lady smack Cheryl. She smacked her back. She just retaliated in self defence as anybody would if they had been punched in the face.' Accused by Lees of lying to protect her bandmate, Nicola retorted, 'I won't lie for anybody. At the end of the day, it's my life, my career. I'm not going to lie for anybody.'

Another witness, Erin Connolly, testified in support of the star. She alleged that Sophie had assaulted her in the lavatories saying, 'A girl let me in front of her and she may have thought I was queue-jumping. She pulled me back hard enough to rip my collar.'

On Friday 17 October, prosecutor Lees urged the jury to remember 'celebrities are not above the law', before they adjourned to consider their verdict. Three days later on Monday 20, after months of turmoil, the jury of seven men and five women returned their verdict to the world – reached by an overwhelming majority of eleven to one. They found Cheryl guilty of assault occasioning actual bodily harm, but cleared her of the additional charge of racially aggravated assault. Judge Richard Howarth described the incident as, 'an unpleasant piece of drunken violence', but added he was surprised Cheryl had 'shown no remorse whatsoever' for the alleged attack. The star gasped and cradled her face in her hands when the verdict was announced.

Lawyer Paul Harris issued a statement on behalf of Cheryl, in which she said she was, 'Thankful that the jury had accepted that this incident has nothing to do with race. I am not a racist and anyone who knows me knows I would not say anything racist,' telling fans she was sorry for the episode. In a bid to quash the rumours surrounding the singer's reportedly unstable position in Girls Aloud, Polydor told the press: 'We are pleased Cheryl has been found not guilty of the main charge against her. In light of this decision, Cheryl's position in Girls Aloud is unaffected.'

The singer was finally acquitted of any counts of racial abuse and could now begin to rebuild her life – but being centre stage during a long and drawn out legal battle had taken its toll on the singer. The star emerged from the courtroom thin and fragile after losing over half a stone due to stress, but relieved she had been cleared of the hurtful allegations of racism. Cheryl was ordered to pay Sophie £500 in compensation, was forced to stump up £3,000 in prosecution costs – and was sentenced to 120 hours of community service. Sophie launched a civil case against the star a month later over Cheryl's failure to apologise for the incident: 'I want the world to see her the way she really is. She is attempting to carry on with her life and ignore what I went through. When I heard what she told the media, it was as if I was being assaulted all over again.' Despite employing the services of high profile lawyer Imran Khan, Sophie decided not to pursue the case any further.

Cheryl carried out the community service in the North East, near to her friends and family who could offer their support during her ordeal. Her tasks included picking up litter and sandpapering benches at the Blue Star football ground in the Woolsington area of Newcastle. In January 2004, a year after the troublesome punch-up, Cheryl finished her community service and decided it was time to celebrate: 'I wanted to get it out of the way. I have learned my lesson now I can look to the future.'

Ever the trooper, Cheryl made her comeback in style – by singing and dancing her way through a five-song set in front of 1,400 cheering fans and mum Joan at Newcastle's Powerhouse club. Opener 'Girls On Film' was greeted with a collective shriek of delight from the crowd, with a seamless segue into hit 'No Good Advice'. The band performed 'Life Got Cold' and 'Jump', before finishing up with 'Sound of The Underground'; all spurred on by the insatiable fans who were ecstatic their local hero was back on form. After the gig, Cheryl admitted it was one of the best nights of her life, adding, 'That was wicked'. Chris Gilroy, manager of the Powerhouse nightclub, admitted it had been a night to remember – with the girls drawing in a never-seen-before crowd at the gay venue. He conceded, 'I have never seen a crowd like it here before. It's been a great success, a real sell-out.'

The star credited her recovery to the unfailing support of her mum Joan, who provided a much-needed shoulder to cry on when the going got tough. She said, 'I've learnt my lesson. It's been a very difficult year, I finished my community service today and I'm looking to the future. My mum has been there for me throughout it all. She has been there and supported me when I have been at my lowest. A lot of stuff has been written and said about me but I have got skin as tough as leather boots. And I think most people take it with a pinch of salt.' And confident the new year was also a fresh start, she vowed to conquer her demons and move on from the incident which had marred her success with Girls Aloud. She added, '2004 is definitely going to be my year. I want to put the past behind me.'

Put the past behind her she most definitely did, but Cheryl admitted her behaviour did reflect badly on the band: 'To be fair, I did let the fans down and I let myself down, really. But give me a second chance. I am supposed to be a role model. I feel sorry for my fans and sorry for my friends and I am sorry for the girls.'

And she admits, over four years after the event, she's still hurt by what she went through. 'I got myself into a bit of a pickle in a nightclub like any normal teenager does. It happens all the time but this was happening, front page national news and that was such a hard time for me. It was so frustrating. I was dealing with all these things at the one time – the fame, the nasty side of fame, really I had to deal with it from the start; the really harsh side of it, not knowing if this was the beginning and the end of my career, just not knowing anything to be honest. It still hurts and I'm still bitter about it to be honest. It can still make me cry, it can still make me feel sick after all this time, so that was hard.'

But Cheryl knows that while time is a great healer, it takes an even greater length of time to shake off negative press: 'I've still got that stigma. I'm still always portrayed like the bitch in the band.'

CHAPTER 9

Nicola's Low-Key Loves

NICOLA ROBERTS MET her childhood sweetheart Carl Egerton while studying Performing Arts at Runcorn Sixth Form College. When Nicola made it into Girls Aloud in November 2002, the couple stayed together, despite having to conduct a long-distance relationship – they had never been apart for longer than two weeks in the past. Carl stayed in Runcorn where he was studying for his A' Levels, while Nicola became initiated into the inner sanctum of pop.

Bombarded with a gaggle of male fans lusting after her, Nicola remained faithful to Carl despite the pressures of fame, and would gush about him at every opportunity. She was in love. 'He's the best looking bloke in the world. He's got a cheeky smile and a great six-pack. We haven't even been apart for two weeks yet and I miss him like mad already.' Nicola found it tough being without Carl by her side, and admitted she felt lonely in his absence: 'I do miss Carl a lot when we're touring or doing the rounds promoting a record.'

Promotional shoots, interview and gigs meant Nicola and the band were constantly busy, and also meeting famous male admirers. Like bandmate Kimberley, rumours abounded she was being romanced by Westlife hunk Mark Feehily – who later admitted he was gay and didn't much care for women. But Nicola was understandably upset by the tabloid gossip linking the pair, and set about letting Carl, who was living with his parents at the time, know he was still the only man for her. 'There's absolutely nothing going on with me and Mark,' she said. 'The first I knew anything about that was when I opened up the paper one morning. I just thought, "Oh my God."' Nicola did her best to reassure her boyfriend the allegations were false: 'I have a boyfriend back home asking me what the hell has been going on. I just told him that it was just a rumour and there was absolutely no truth in it. Fortunately, he believed me.' She added the experience hadn't damaged their relationship, and was keen to point out Carl was always there for her, lending her moral support since day one. 'Carl has been behind me all the way,' she explained. 'He's just as excited as I am. He isn't paranoid and he knows this is my career and that it's what I've always wanted to do. He supports me in that. He trusts me.'

Having a partner who knew her before she became famous was important for Nicola. She enjoyed being able to keep out of the public eye if she wanted to, unlike her bandmates who were being romanced by celebrities. 'I was with him before the band started and we are just the same now, if not stronger than ever,' she said. 'Our relationship is just like any other relationship. My boyfriend comes from where I grew up and although he is not in the business, he loves the music scene. I can keep my private life private which is the way I like it.'

While living in London, Nicola learned the side effect of conducting a long distance relationship – extortionately high phone bills. She would spend colossal amounts of money every month keeping in touch with Carl, sending numerous text messages of love and making never-ending phone calls to help cope with the distance between them. 'We have to keep in touch on the phone,' she explained. 'I don't think about what it costs because I just want to talk to him. Then at the end of the month, my bill's absolutely massive. On average, I'm running up at least £400 every month – calling or texting Carl. We text each other constantly, 20 times a day.'

As soon as Carl's exams were over, he took the opportunity to travel down to north London to visit Nicola – and soon became a hit with Cheryl, Nadine, Kimberley and Sarah, who enjoyed having a man around the house: 'Carl isn't working at the moment so he has been helping with things in the house I share with the other girls in London. He's very handy. He gets on well with all the girls and joins us to party whenever he can – he's like the sixth band member.'

However in March 2004, it looked like it was all over

for love's young dream. Nicola and Carl split when the pressure of Girls Aloud's success became too much to handle – but not being with each other became an even bigger difficulty for the couple, and they reconciled just three months later in June of the same year. Nicola and Carl would be photographed together at showbiz parties and events looking lovingly at one another and getting down to some serious smooching, and it seemed as if the couple were destined to be together forever. But after a five year relationship, the pair parted ways in December 2006, blaming the pressures of work and Girls Aloud's hectic schedule for their split.

Bandmate and best pal Cheryl thought Nicola and Carl's split was for the best, as Nicola had been in a steady relationship since hitting 16, and was too young to settle down. 'They've been together since they were 16, but she needs to do a bit of living,' she said. 'Nicola's probably one of the wildest girls in the band.' While Nicola boogied her way around the Newz bar in Liverpool and a plethora of London celebrity hangouts, another Carl was quick to catch her eye. Nicola wasn't going to be enjoying the single life for long.

She hooked up with another fellow northerner, Carl Davis, and was soon smitten. The pair had a high profile row at the *NME* Awards the same month, which Nicola attended with Sarah as they were presenting an award. Carl allegedly called Nicola 'a divvy,' to which she was not best pleased, and their feud made the gossip pages of the tabloids the following day. They soon kissed and made up, stepping out together on the social scene on countless occasions, including Sugababe Amelle Berrabah's 23rd birthday celebration at swish London club Silver in April. But Nicola is reluctant to speak to the press about the relationship, telling reporters, 'It's early days and he's a nice Scouse lad.'

CHAPTER 10

Kimberley's Chemisty

WHEN IT COMES to love and romance, Kimberley blossomed early, sharing her first kiss with a boy friend while still at school. She says, 'It wasn't awful or anything. It was with a boy I had fancied for ages who started going to the same stage school as me, I must have been about 12 or 13.'

When Kimberley hit the big time with *Popstars: The Rivals* and Girls Aloud, she was dating Stockport County footballer Martin Pemberton, who she had been seeing for over two years. However, manager Louis Walsh attempted to throw a spanner into the romantic workings of his female charges by vowing none of his girl band would date unsuitable types – namely footballers and fellow popstars. 'Louis has said he doesn't want his girls dating footballers or popstars – well, it's a little bit late for that,' said Kim. Kimberley conceded she found being in a relationship with Pemberton amusing, as the footballer/popstar love match is a much hackneyed cliché: 'We have a laugh about our relationship. It's quite corny, a footballer and a pop star.' But Kimberley wasn't keen on styling her relationship as the next Victoria and David Beckham. 'People keep asking me that and it's a bit stupid, really,' she said. 'I never think of us like that. Posh and Becks are on a completely different level to us. I love them as much as the next person and doubt anyone could compete.'

Kimberley and fellow Bradfordian Martin, who was five years her senior, met for the first time on a night out in a club in Leeds, and instantly fell for one another. 'I thought he was gorgeous the first time I saw him,' Kimberley explains. 'I can't believe we've been together for this long. But Martin is really special, he's so supportive of me. I knew Martin before he became a footballer and we both had these big dreams. You connect with someone or you don't. Everything about you and the person fits together. And you can't put your finger on it, you just know.' The singer didn't plan on tying the knot, but did believe Pemberton was The One: 'I'm only 21 and don't want to get married yet. I'm happy the way I am at the moment, but I think he's The One for me. Definitely.'

But as Girls Aloud's musical inertia kept them moving forward full steam ahead, things were beginning to look a little shaky for the pair. With Martin up north and Kimberley down south in London, they were forced to conduct a long-distance relationship; however the pop star was confident they could work through the difficult times: 'I don't get to see Martin very often. But when you've got a relationship that's so solid it's not as hard as people think to keep it going. You've just got to make more effort. And, if you both want it to work, then you make that effort, so we don't find it difficult.' While Martin came to cheer on his girlfriend at an ever increasing series of gigs and promotional commitments, Kimberley found it tough to get the time off to watch her beau excel in his field of work. 'Since being in the band,' Kimberley explained, 'I haven't had the chance to watch him play football, and I feel a bit bad about that.'

Sadly, things fell apart at the beginning of 2004 and the couple split in February due to the pair's hectic schedule. Kimberley admitted, 'We hardly saw each other to be fair. We were both really busy with work and that meant when we saw each other we took it out on each other. We thought it best to cut our losses and go our separate ways. We are still on speaking terms.'

After the mutual break-up, Kimberley threw herself into recording Girls Aloud's new album in a bid to take her mind off men. It was a tough time for the group, as relationships were ending for the other girls around the same time. Cheryl explained, 'We're not even thinking about men now – we've got each other and that's enough for us. Everyone thinks you need to be going out with a man to have a good time, but that's rubbish. We feel like the girls in *Sex and The City* – but without the sex. We're strong and independent and are doing just fine without blokes.'

Later that year, however, Kimberley was ready to once

again look for love, telling a local newspaper: 'I want to find someone who can make me laugh and is fun to be around, so it's more about personality. He would have to be quiet but confident and have some intrigue about him. I don't like guys who give everything away.'

In May 2004, Kimberley was linked with Ray Panthaki, who at the time played Ronny Ferreira in BBC soap *Eastenders*, and in December that year, Mark Feehily from Westlife. The tabloids claimed the couple hooked up after the Irish group's performance at London's G-A-Y and swapped numbers after getting on 'extremely well' together. Red faces all round at the UK's gossip columns then, when Feehily came out in August 2005 after admitting he had kept his sexuality hidden for the duration of his tenure with Westlife.

The same year, Kimberley met Justin Scott, of now-defunct boy band Triple 8. Girls Aloud and Triple 8 shared the same record label, Polydor, and the pair would bump into one another at gigs and events, and became firm friends. Not long after, Kimberley and Justin realised their relationship was more than just friendship, and began dating. Justin admits he fancied Kimberley even before they met. 'I actually first fell for Kim when I was watching *Popstars: The Rivals*,' he says. 'Even before she got picked for the band. I just thought, "Wow, she's nice."'

The couple were determined to keep themselves to themselves, and avoided high-profile events and parties as they much preferred staying in of an evening than hitting the tiles at the latest swanky venue in town.

Kimberley says, 'We didn't want the pressure of other people looking at our relationship. But now it just works between us. We don't like going to those showbiz parties and premieres anyway. We'd rather go to our local cinema and get some pick 'n' mix like normal people.'

The pair soon moved in together, and share a swanky London flat. Kimberley admits she gets on well with Justin's nine-year-old daughter Chloe, who lives in Bristol, but admits it's not the right time for marriage: 'I still feel quite young and everything's so hectic with the band. I might save marriage and kids until I can concentrate on it more.'

CHAPTER 11

Nadine, the not-so-Desperate Housewife

NADINE HAD BEEN dating Derry boy and Charlton Athletic footballer Neil McCafferty for over two years before winning her place in Girls Aloud. The pair met at a youth club disco in the city, and even at 15 years of age, Nadine was something of a head-turner. 'We fell for each other straight away. Neil has just confessed to me recently that when he first saw me at the disco, he had to take a second look because he was so impressed,' Nadine recalled.

She was well-versed in the etiquette of conducting a long-distance relationship, as Neil was based in England with the team for most of the football season while she was in Derry, making another bid for stardom after the Irish Popstars controversy. 'We don't get to see each other much but we're on the telephone all the time,' she said. 'Neil's just brilliant, he's so supportive of everything

I do. I've been going out with him for ages and things just keep getting better.'

In November 2002, the spotlight of fame was thrust upon Nadine. Now both Neil and Nadine had busy schedules, and the singer admits it was difficult adjusting to the changes, especially as they found it hard to regularly see one another. But the couple kept in touch by phone, and endeavoured to meet up whenever they could. 'We keep in touch by calling each other a few times a day and we're always texting each other too,' said Nadine, who is the first to admit she's not a romantic at heart. 'I'm not an overly romantic person and I don't send flowers and things like that. Maybe he should be sending them to me though.' During *Popstars: The Rivals*, Nadine was linked with male contestant Matt Johnston, which Neil understandably found hard to stomach. Matt alleged he was 'having a bit of fun' with Nadine, and that they spoke on the phone 'all the time', and Neil was not best pleased. Nadine was also linked with Triple 8 star and Polydor labelmate David Wilcox while she was seeing Neil. Speaking in 2004, Nadine said, 'When I was with Neil I found that it was hard for him to read that I had gone off with other blokes even though I hadn't.' One crush Neil didn't mind his girlfriend revealing was her love for the then-Celtic boss Martin O'Neill. 'He is so passionate about the game and that's what I like to see in a man,' she said. 'Neil is a big Celtic fan too. So you never know, I could maybe have a word with Martin if I ever meet him.'

Just before Christmas 2003, Neil and Nadine agreed

to split. The pressure of their high-profile long-distance relationship had become too stressful and their was no choice but to end it. 'It's over between us now,' said Nadine. 'We have been together since I was 15 so it was going to end at some stage. But I still love Neil, he was my first love. I am over the initial shock of it now, but we are still really good friends and are still speaking. We still care about each other but the romance just fizzled out.'

Nadine was glad to be living the single life, but was daunted at the prospect of being 'on her own'. Luckily Cheryl was there to lend her support, and the pair planned to celebrate Valentine's Day together. 'My bandmate Cheryl Tweedy is single as well so I've got somebody to be with. This will be her second Valentine's Day single so we are going to buy each other a Valentine's card.' Nadine vowed to enjoy her new found freedom: 'I'm going to concentrate on enjoying myself now and going out loads. There's always that possibility you might meet someone exciting.' But she was still frightened of becoming a spinster: 'I have these nightmares that I will be in my 30s and still looking for love – but I've got a bit of time yet. Like every girl I want to settle down some day and have a great husband and kids.' In the interim, however, Nadine was happy to throw herself into her career and have fun: 'I've swore off men and am going to concentrate on my job and enjoying my life.'

Girls Aloud fans were delighted by Nadine's new single status, sending fan mail filled with marriage proposals and offers of hot dates to the singer – all of which she politely declined. She says, 'You get up to 100 letters each week and most of them include photos. But you could never meet anyone that you don't know properly. Most of the letters are very sweet. A few guys have proposed marriage and all the rest of it but I don't take any of it too seriously.' Nadine didn't plan on settling down again in a hurry – but reckoned her next serious relationship would be with The One. 'I don't want a serious relationship. I went out with my ex Neil for nearly three years. I don't think I'll have another long romance like that until I'm ready to get married.' She wasn't planning on becoming a serial dater as she was wary of kiss-and-tells after bandmates Cheryl and Sarah both experienced ex-boyfriends selling their stories to the tabloids. 'I guess you can't sleep around with randoms unless you are 100 per cent sure of them. But then you wouldn't want to sleep with someone you half know anyway. You can get really hung up on it and think that he's only talking to you because you're in a band. I'm not the kind of girl to sleep around – I'm too shy.'

Nadine knew what she wanted in a man, telling the press she 'wanted a boyfriend with a Derry accent – or Irish at least', that she thought Irish actor Colin Farrell was 'gorgeous', and that while she wasn't looking for a serious relationship, 'if the gardener from *Desperate Housewives* were to ask me out I wouldn't say no.' Little did she know this would turn out to be a precursor of what was to come. She was linked with Irish footballer Robbie Keane, singer Robbie Williams and wrongly rumoured to be dating Girls Aloud backing dancer

Stephen Walker, but admitted she was often approached by hordes of men she wasn't at all interested in: 'Guys come up to me and try their luck and all at nightclubs but I always send them packing.' She rekindled her romance briefly with Neil, but insisted the pair were 'more friends than anything. I don't see him as much as I'd see a regular boyfriend.'

She vowed that 2006 would be the year she would find a man, although she knew it would be tough, being one fifth of the UK's best and biggest girl band. She said, 'I just don't get the time to meet the right guy and it just keeps getting harder. I really do miss the emotional bond of a proper relationship. My biggest priority is to find a decent guy, if there is one out there. I've decided that 2006 could be my lucky year and I could find Mr Right. It's much harder finding a man than you would imagine. I'm always touring and working so there's little time to look for love.'

Ironically, it was during touring and Girls Aloud-related commitments that Nadine met her dream man. A ten-day promotional visit to Australia at the beginning of 2006 saw a chance meeting with *Desperate Housewives* star Jesse Metcalfe. At the time, Nadine said, 'I've fancied him for ages, and he's a babe.' The pair met in a Sydney bar, with Jesse asking Nadine for her number – but after leaving, he realised he had taken her contact details down wrongly. 'Nadine actually came up to our group,' said Jesse. 'I could tell straight away she wasn't the type to fall for cheesy chat-up lines. I was just trying to play it cool with her and it seems like it worked.' Jesse searched the hotels in the area to find out where she was staying, finally tracking her down to the Four Seasons hotel and sent her some flowers and left a message to call him. Jesse was smitten: 'I was struck by the way she played it so cool, the way she carries herself – she's definitely a lady. She has a lot of respect for herself. Right after the first night we hung out I knew I wanted to spend more time with her.' Nadine played hard to get initially, taking time to get in contact with the actor. But soon enough, Nadine came round and the pair talked on the phone for a month and a half before Jesse came to the UK to visit her.

It seemed as if the pair were the acting and music world's golden couple. They were both gorgeous, talented, and devoted to each other. They would speak on the phone five times a day, although Nadine admitted the time difference between London and Los Angeles was sometimes difficult. 'Sometimes you're not on the same wavelength when you speak on the phone,' she explained. 'Like I will have been out and I might be drunk and he'll be out shopping.' Nadine racked up thousands of air miles visiting Jesse in LA, while he would travel to the UK, and his girlfriend's hometown of Derry to meet the Coyle clan in August 2006 – so daunting a task he felt the need to down a few sneaky drinks before the introduction: 'The first time I met Nadine's mum and dad I was very drunk! But it seemed they warmed to me. I don't think the Irish frown upon having a drink. Nadine's family are really cool people.' It's certainly not every day a Hollywood A-Lister treads on Northern Irish turf, so it really was something special for both Nadine and the people of Northern Ireland, who took Jesse to their hearts as an adopted son. Jesse watched on lovingly at Girls Aloud gigs, and even admitted to liking his girlfriend's music – even though pop wasn't his favourite musical genre: 'I'm not the biggest fan of pop music but it's catchy stuff – I find myself humming it in the shower.'

But in November 2006, Jesse allegedly dumped Nadine, who flew out to California to salvage her relationship with the star. The couple later branded the split 'a minor break'. 'It wasn't really a split,' says Nadine, 'It was blown out of proportion. People have arguments, it's a fact, and sometimes after a row you just want to be left alone. But it wasn't as dramatic as people made it out to be. I mean, we were talking all the way through and talking about us splitting up.' After the reconciliation, Jesse spent Christmas in Northern Ireland with Nadine's family, even helping out at a charity race in Greencastle, Tyrone in December.

Nadine even hinted she would move to the States in order to be with Jesse, with rumours abounding her parents Niall and Lillian were looking into opening a bar across the Atlantic. Niall said, 'We are looking at the idea of opening an Irish bar on the beach and turning it into a big success. We want to serve all the traditional food and have a good sing-song every night. Nadine might even pop in every now and again to sing. Nadine is really excited about the idea and loves the lifestyle over there. I'm heading over to California in a few weeks to organise things and make a final decision.' It seemed as if Nadine – and perhaps her family – would move to LA to be with Jesse full time. 'I would love to live in the States,' she said. 'I really like the lifestyle. But I really like London. I love the girls, I love being in the band. But I'm greedy and like the best of everything. But who knows what will happen?' The press enjoyed perpetuating rumours Jesse and Nadine were just days from getting engaged, although the couple always denied they were ready to tie the knot.

In an interview with *OK!* Magazine in March 2007, it was clear that the pressure of a transatlantic relationship was beginning to take its toll. 'I have to admit it's challenging,' said Jesse, 'Even when you're seeing someone close by it's tough. And you sometimes misunderstand each other on the phone. I know that about two weeks is my limit for being apart from Nadine. I start to get a little weird.' It was a swift change in attitude for Jesse, who at the beginning of their relationship had boasted he enjoyed conducting a long distance relationship with the singer. He said, 'I like a confident girl who knows her mind and has something going on in her life. That creates a little separation, which is healthy for a relationship. You don't want a girl who is going to glue onto your life and become too needy. I like a girl who is independent.'

Things would go from bad to worse for the couple just weeks after their early March 12-page declaration of love in Hawaii in *OK*! Magazine,when Jesse checked himself into rehab after a four-day bender in LA, when he visited four clubs in the space of an evening and was thrown out of a Hollywood hotel for abusing a doorman. Nadine was in pieces, but vowed to support her man during his stay in Promises Treatment Centre in Malibu, California – where Britney Spears had recently spent her rehab tenure – for 'alcohol issues'. Nadine's dad Niall said, 'We saw Jesse regularly when we were in the US and we often thought he drank less than us. Nadine is devastated this has happened and blames herself that she didn't see the warning signs. She's a sensitive girl and it's going to break her heart that she has commitments in London while he is dealing with this. Nadine is in total shock. She never saw this coming, and neither did we.'

Nadine flew to Los Angeles upon Jesse's completion of the rehab programme, spending five days with him before coming back to the UK. She told the press, 'He's fine, he's doing really well. It was so lovely to see him. Jesse is getting help. I'm just glad he has realised he can't go on the way he was. It was hurting me seeing him do that to himself. I'm going to be there for him and do all I can to help. But at the end of the day, Jesse has to make the decisions to stop on his own.'

Just days after Nadine's glowing report from California, Jesse was papped holding hands with and hugging a mystery lady. For Nadine, it was the final straw, and she dumped the star almost immediately and vowed to find another suitor. She reportedly told the press, 'It's over between Jesse and me. I'm not the kind of girl to put up with nonsense like that. I'll meet the right person when the time is right. I'm disappointed, but what can I do. There's no point in hanging on when it's gets to this stage.' Speculation attributed the cause of the split to Jesse's philandering ways, although the tabloids would later allege the actor's 'immense jealousy' had let to his unceremonious dumping. During their relationship, Nadine had admitted Jesse often got jealous when she received attention from other men: 'He's really protective of me and hates it when guys talk to me, even though there is nothing funny going on. I don't get jealous when girls talk to him because that's part of his job and he's in the public eye.' Unsurprisingly for such an in-demand stunning girl, *Daily Star* columnist – and Sarah's other half at the time – Joe Mott hinted at the end of April that Nadine had already found a 'superior replacement' for bad-boy Jesse.

CHAPTER 12

Sarah's Hunks (and Hack)

GETTING INTO GIRLS Aloud was something of a double-edged sword for Sarah. While she had finally seen her dreams of singing stardom realised, having her love life under the constant scrutiny of the press really took its toll. She had entered the competition while dating mechanic John Turnbull, one year her senior, but their two-year relationship soon buckled under the strains of her new found fame. 'When I first started doing this I was with someone who didn't really understand it all,' she later explained. 'It was a little bit difficult for them to accept what I was doing and the attention what I was doing received. If I wasn't in this industry and I was going out with someone who was, I think you would feel a little bit alienated.'

She fell into the arms of fellow *Popstars: The Rivals* contestant Mikey Green, who made it to the final 10, but was voted off before the boys were narrowed down to five – the bunch who would make up One True Voice. Both being in the public eye helped to bring them together, as Mikey had recently split from his girlfriend. Sarah and Mikey got together in December 2002 after sharing a smooch at a Christmas party. 'His relationship fell apart because his girlfriend didn't understand the pressures on him,' explained Sarah. 'And I had the same thing with the guy I was seeing. So, we had a lot in common.' Another thing the couple had in common was their hometown – yet despite living five minutes away from each other in Manchester, and sharing the same group of friends, they were brought together by the show. 'We literally lived around the corner from each other but never met,' Sarah says. 'We didn't know each other but had loads of mutual friends which was really weird.'

Sarah was smitten with Mikey, who soon moved into her London flat in April 2003. She branded him 'my soulmate and best friend', and believed their meeting was down to fate – and told a journalist that 'yes, he could be The One'. A few months later in August, Mikey and his band Phixx – formed from the five boys who didn't make it into One True Voice, who had now disbanded – were offered a £500,000 three-album deal. What the couple got up to in the bedroom was a constant source of interest to the tabloids, who regaled their readers with tales of the pair's sex life. From fancy firemen outfits to diamond encrusted whips, it was even alleged a neighbour had slipped a note under Sarah's front door saying, 'If you're having sex the whole world doesn't need to know about it.' But it wasn't just a physical attraction between the pair – it was also a meeting of minds. The fact both Sarah and Mikey were in the same industry only served to bolster their relationship. Reports linked Sarah to Polydor labelmate Triple 8's Josh Barnett, but it proved to be unfounded. 'Any bloke could get intimidated if their girlfriend was in this industry and got approached by other people within the industry,' said Sarah. 'But we trust each other 110 per cent. We won't let anything get in our way – tabloids or bad press or anything.'

Sarah's world would be shaken up in October 2003 when her ex John sold his story to the *News Of The World,* bemoaning the fact both lived at home with their parents during their relationship, describing in detail the pair's sexual exploits on cricket pitches and phone boxes – and even claimed he was still 'really good mates' with the singer. Sarah was devastated. She had trusted John, and thought he would have been the last person in the world to approach the tabloids with a kiss-and-tell. She said, 'Before Mikey I went out with someone for five years but he sold a story about me. Of all the people, I didn't think he would betray me. He had pictures from when we were on holiday – he's the only person who ever took topless pictures of me. I'd known him 10 years and trusted him totally. I just couldn't believe he would double-cross me like that.'

In January 2004, just over a year after they got together, Sarah and Mikey had a trial separation, and he moved out of their shared flat. But it was clear the couple couldn't bear to be apart from one another, and had soon rekindled their relationship. Just under five months later in June, however, the pair once again went their separate ways – and this time it was for good. They had had a tough time dealing with press interest in the daily dealings of their love, and had been forced apart. Sarah later explained, 'The beginning of our relationship was great because there was no pressure, but as soon as the spotlight was on us it made things difficult. When you're away from each other a lot it does put a strain on things. The arguments start to creep in, little bits start appearing in the press and in the end it was better to just go our separate ways.' Speaking in 2007, Sarah admitted she was still in contact with Mikey, but the intensity of their relationship had made it difficult for them to remain friends. 'We still speak every so often,' she explained, 'but when you have something that deep with someone and you try to stay friends, it can be difficult.'

Gorgeous Sarah was always going to be a hit with the male species, and after her relationship with Mikey ended, men all over the country got rather excitable. While Sarah was devastated by the break up, she embarked on a one-woman mission to enjoy the single life – with a few snogs shared with the opposite sex thrown in. Around the same time as her split from Mikey, Sarah was linked with professional ladies' man Calum Best, son of legendary Northern Ireland and Manchester United footballer George Best. The pair had a short-lived but tempestuous relationship, and the couple soon split in August 2004, though remained close friends.

Sarah says, 'When I realised I couldn't change him, I

realised our relationship couldn't carry on. It would have got very destructive and we wouldn't be friends now. We have a very tempestuous relationship. We bicker all the time, but that's part of our nature, we are both very stubborn. Nobody will ever understand how tough it was with Calum. I've looked at the inner Calum and it frightened him. It's every man's dream to be where he is – he can walk into clubs and just walk out with most women. With me, Calum realised he had someone to talk to – I wasn't one of those girls who just fell at his feet.' But Sarah vowed to find another man, and immersed herself in the task in hand: 'I guess I'll have to kiss a lot of frogs before I find my prince – and Calum is definitely a frog.'

In May 2005, Sarah was rumoured to have rekindled her romance with old flame Mikey Green, but just a few months later in August, serial dater Sarah was linked with Welsh *T4* presenter Steve Jones. Girls Aloud had appeared on the show to promote their new single 'Long Hot Summer', and the pair immediately hit it off.

Sarah's friendship with Calum came to the fore when his father died in December 2005, after a long battle with alcohol addiction. She admitted she wanted to support Calum so he wouldn't end up following the same self-destructive path as George. She spoke to him every day following his father's death, and considered flying to the funeral in Belfast but couldn't get the time off work. 'I would have loved to have been in Belfast to lend him some support on such a very sad day,' she said. 'I met George and he was a very nice man.'

After months of partying and throwing caution to the testosterone-heavy wind, Sarah found herself linked with a whole host of A-List males, including Jennifer Lopez's ex-husband Cris Judd. Sarah was evidently enjoying the single life: 'I used to like being in a relationship so I'd go straight out of one and into another relationship. I've never had time to be on my own and just enjoy it.' Months later she was in the arms of Hollywood star Stephen Dorff. The pair dated briefly in June 2006, with the actor coming to see Sarah and Girls Aloud perform a gig at Wembley Arena during their *Chemistry* tour. It didn't last long, as his wild ways were a bit too much for Sarah. She says, 'We just had a bit of a snog. He was a lot better looking in *Blade*. He's a good looking guy, but he's certainly not someone who wants to settle down.' In July and August the same year she was once again linked with old flame Steve Jones, and after Cheryl's wedding in July, she was rumoured to be seeing footballer and Ashley Cole's best man, Barnet player Paolo Vernazza, who she allegedly hooked up with at her pal's big day. Sarah's friend Katie Price also tried to get in on the matchmaking act, attempting to set her up with her brother Mike. But it didn't work out: 'Oh I love Katie so much. She did try. Mike's lovely but I wasn't ready for that. And who knew what was around the corner.'

But Sarah was beginning to get bored of her partying ways, and wanted to find a decent man to share her life with: 'I've always had a thing for a bad boy, and you really do think you can change them. But you can't unless they want to.' And she insisted she wasn't the man magnet the papers had made her out to be. 'I have this reputation of having tonnes of men,' she lamented, 'but I have only ever had three real boyfriends. And they have all been trouble. I seem to have a radar for shits.' Sarah yearned for a boyfriend. 'I'm at the point where I'm sick of actually enjoying being single,' she said. 'I want to have someone to share things with now. I'm sick of going to the same clubs. I like going out, I love socialising but I hate going to the same sort of places, same faces, same hangovers. It would be nice to have someone to have nights in with and watch DVDs and order takeaways. I just want a boyfriend. I'm not saying it has to be The One but I wouldn't mind having a boyfriend.'

She admitted her experience with Mikey had changed her attitude to relationships. She confessed she though he 'was the guy I thought I would have married', and that she hadn't felt the same way for anyone else since they split. She explained, 'I am so wary about getting involved with someone again because it's horrible when it all comes to an end. Before I used to go out with people and hear wedding bells straight away, but now it's different. I take my relationships seriously. I'm not one of these "here today, gone tomorrow" kind of people.'

Months later, Sarah confessed she was fed up with men, and knew she had to employ different tactics if she was to find a man she wanted to date: 'I'm so sick of men. I'm so bitter and twisted, and I don't go out with the intention of pulling. You're never going to meet the man of your dreams in a nightclub anyway,' adding she was putting her days of going for cute men behind her:

'I'm over the pretty boys now, they're a bunch of twats,' In March 2006, Sarah's mum Marie confessed she wanted to see her daughter on the arm of a gentleman, and not an endless list of ne'er do well lotharios in the vein of her past conquests. 'I really do want a nice boy for Sarah,' she said. 'The public image is of a bit of a party girl, but underneath that she's extremely sensitive and caring and loving and intelligent and if anyone actually takes time to get to know her they'll see that side of her.'

One man did take the time to get to know her, and in November 2006, Sarah began dating *Daily Star* gossip columnist Joe Mott after years of friendship – and one previous rebuttal. 'Our friendship has just gone from that to talking on the phone a lot to this. We went out one night and I was with Joe,' she explains, 'and I looked at him and thought, "okay!". I mean, I knew years ago he'd tried to get my number but then I was like, "No way am I dating a journalist" and wouldn't give it as I didn't know him well enough. It took him two years of hard work to persuade me to go out with him.' Sarah admits there was chemistry between the pair, which helped her make the decision to finally give in and allow Joe to have her number. She claimed that with curly-haired hack Joe, she'd abandoned the hunks of her past and was concentrating on companionship. 'It's about being on the same level. You can go out with the best looking person on the planet and there could be nothing in their head. What's the point in going out with a beautiful shell? I need intellectual stimulation.'

Famed for her partying ways and penchant for unsuitable men, Sarah believed her relationship with Mott had changed her for the better – and her bandmates all agreed. 'She has become like a normal human being!' says Cheryl. 'Before she was just a party wild child.' Kimberley added, 'He's calmed her down a hell of a lot. We always knew there was a little something between them.' Despite the unorthodox pairing of a celebrity and someone who makes his living from writing about celebrities, Sarah appeared to have blossomed with her new man. 'If he had have been a bad sort, I'm sure I would have been warned off before now. I think Joe saved me from myself because I wasn't in the best of places last year,' she explained. 'Working hard and being single took its toll.' But she admited a wedding wasn't on the cards just yet, and was simply enjoying her new found couple-dom: 'I can't see myself getting married until way after the band is over. I don't want to jinx it by saying it's going to work out with Joe in the long run, but things are ticking over nicely.' Sadly, Matt and Harding parted ways in May 2007, and Sarah is now enjoying her single-status once again.

CHAPTER 13

Cheryl's Path to WAG-dom

WHEN CHERYL RECEIVED a call back for the Popstars: The Rivals auditions in London, she didn't just get into the final 30, but she also landed herself a boyfriend. While she admitted at one stage she wasn't interested in having a bloke – 'I went out with the best-looking lad at school but it only lasted for a week,' she explained. 'I was too interested in hanging out with the girls,' – someone had caught the 19-year-old's eye.

After breaking up with boyfriend Richard Sweeney before embarking on the *Popstars: The Rivals* auditions, she was young, free and single. Sweeney later said, 'Cheryl is a lovely girl. She has always wanted to be where she is now. She has been through rough times and now she is living her dream. I wish her all the best.' She was smitten with fellow contestant and former carpet fitter Jacob Thompson – who was famously advised to remove his decorative facial hair à la Craig David by the judges, or risk not being taken seriously as a pop star. A spokesperson for the programme confirmed the romance to the tabloids, saying, 'Love did blossom at the London call-back in August and the pair have been seeing each other ever since.'

Cheryl and Leicester lad Jacob conducted their relationship under the glare of the nascent showbiz spotlight from August, but disaster befell the couple when Jacob failed to make the final 20 – but Cheryl's dreams of pop stardom were still very much alive, and the pair soon split in October 2002. After the break up, Cheryl said she was disappointed she hadn't had the opportunity to get to know Jacob better. 'I thought he was lovely,' she confessed. 'His eyelashes are amazing and I love his light eyes and dark skin. He's got a fantastic body. We text but we don't have the time to see each other any more. We didn't get a chance to get to know each other properly.'

Even though she wasn't yet an established star, former boyfriends began to come out of the woodwork to inform the press of Cheryl's past sexual exploits. Plumber Steve Thornton sold his story to the *News Of The World* in October, upsetting Cheryl at an already stressful time. They had met in a Newcastle café where the Geordie worked as a teenager, and soon began dating – and did so for five months. Steve told the paper of their sexual activities in great detail, explaining how they got intimate in her sister Gillian's flat and his rude preferences for Cheryl dressing in cowgirl gear. 'The worst thing is you can't defend yourself [against kiss-and-tell stories],' she says. 'You just have to get a tougher skin, laugh it off. But I was so upset and so hurt, because he treated me like shit the whole time I was seeing him, and then this . . . I rang him and said, "I want an explanation, because all I ever did was help and support you." He started crying and said they'd been hounding him for 10 months.'

In December 2002, when she was revealed as a member of the newly-formed Girls Aloud, she struck up a friendship with former Ultimate Kaos member Haydon Eshun. Cheryl had been a huge fan of the teen boy band in the mid 1990s. She insisted the pair were friends, but rumours abounded the relationship was a lot more serious. According to one newspaper, Haydon racked up a £1,300 phone bill keeping in touch with Cheryl while he was filming musical has-been reality TV show, *Reborn In The USA*. The couple were spotted in swanky west London hotel K-West, and allegedly became more than just friends – although Cheryl played it down, saying, 'I was obsessed with him when I was nine. We've become friends but I'm still single.' But the reported 'relationship' wasn't to last long, and soon Haydon and Cheryl were back to being mates. Haydon said, 'I really like Cheryl. We haven't got back together but who knows what's going to happen in the future? She is such a great girl and she's got a wicked smile.'

It wasn't long before Cheryl was being hunted down by showbusiness' most prolific lotharios. Duncan James from Blue was desperate to take the singer out on a date after meeting her during filming for *Popstars: The Rivals*, but she wasn't interested, nonchalantly giving the star the brush off. 'Apparently Duncan fancies me and that's flattering,' she said. 'Every teenage girl wants to go out with him but I'd say "No."' In March 2003, she was linked with Anthony Scott-Lee of short-lived boy band 3SL, brother of former Steps star Lisa Scott-Lee. A few months later, a potential boyfriend appeared in the least likely place – in the family of a fellow Girls Aloud-er.

Cheryl met Kimberley's brother Adam on a visit to the Walsh family's hometown of Bradford, and was instantly smitten. She had fallen for the student, who she dubbed 'a male version of me'. 'I feel really homesick at the moment,' she explained, 'but it's been helped since I met Kimberley's brother. We'd never met before but we just clicked and everything's going great. He's like the male version of me and we're getting along just fine! Although he's living in Yorkshire and I'm always on the road, it hasn't been too much of a nightmare to see him.' The couple would double date with Kimberley and her then-boyfriend Martin Pemberton, much to the amusement of their friends. Kimberley admitted she was apprehensive about the love match, as she risked losing a friend and a brother: 'It's hard because they're two people I really love, so if anything goes wrong it's going to be awful.' The couple did eventually split in September that year after four months together, but things didn't appear to be at all acrimonious.

But Cheryl wasn't happy. She lamented her single status, as Nicola, Nadine, Sarah and Kimberley all had boyfriends, and the Geordie believed she would never find the perfect man. At one point, Sarah allegedly offered – albeit jokingly – to sleep with her fellow bandmate if she didn't find a man before the end of 2003. Cheryl said, 'The others found Mr Right before Girls Aloud took off. It's impossible for me to start a relationship. We are working so hard there's no opportunity to meet someone.' She lamented the lack of men brave enough to make the first move: 'I never get chatted up – it's really frustrating. I want a bloke with hidden charms but I only get approached by the cocky idiots who swagger around like God's gift thinking they're brill. My ideal man would be 50 Cent – I wouldn't mind breeding a whole football team with him. But I would be just as happy with a builder or a postie – as long as he was a Geordie.'

It was a difficult time for the star, and not just in the romance stakes, as she had been accused of assaulting a toilet attendant in January. Her trial began in October, and finding a boyfriend was the last thing on her mind. But in the midst of the court proceedings, Cheryl was linked with her tour manager, 34-year-old Drew Lyall, who had provided a shoulder to cry on and had been a trusted confidant during the tough spell in the singer's life. However, a spokesman for the singer said at the time: 'Cheryl and Drew are good friends. He's been really supportive.'

At the close of the girls' first year together, Cheryl was linked with Newcastle United striker Kieron Dyer. The romance was to be short-lived, with the pair parting only a few weeks later. Speaking at the time, Cheryl said, 'I have no time for romance. My career comes first and all my time is spent concentrating on that. I want to put the past behind me.' Concentrate on the band she did, but she was still on the lookout for The One. But she was perplexed as to why she didn't get as many offers of love as she would have liked: 'I don't know what it is but boys are too scared to approach me.'

That would all change towards the close of 2004. Cheryl, Nadine, Nicola and Kimberley moved into a swish London apartment complex, which incidentally also housed a number of top names from the worlds of showbiz and sport. It was here England footballer Ashley Cole, who was then playing for Arsenal, spied the singer and made it his mission to ask her out on a date in October. It was love at first sight for the sportsman. Ashley later admitted, 'It sounds cheesy but from the first time I saw her at the tennis court I knew that I would be with her for the rest of my life.' But Cheryl had other ideas. She says, 'The first time I met him he was at his mate's flat, near where I lived in north London. I walked past the window and he shouted, "Hey, hot lips" and, "Nice bum". I hate stuff like that, so I rolled my eyes and was, like, "Piss off."' But Ashley resolved to do everything in his power to get his woman. He explains, 'She bombed me out at the first chance when I asked for her number. But as Arsene Wenger (Ashley's manager at Arsenal) always says to me, "Stay touch-tight and you'll get your man" – or girl.'

Cheryl admits she didn't feel the time was right to be

considering potential boyfriends, and despite turning down Ashley's offer of a date, she found herself falling for the footballer – and even found her impending love written in the stars: 'The more I saw him in the papers, the more I just couldn't stop thinking about him. Then I went to see a psychic in Newcastle and he said, "You've been looking at this guy in a magazine." And I had been. We started seeing each other, and we really hit it off. I wasn't looking for a relationship when I met Ashley and certainly not a long term one, but pretty soon after I met him I knew something was different and I knew I had never felt like that before.' Cheryl wasn't going to let her past experience of romance cloud her judgement on Ashley, and threw herself into the pairing with abandon. 'I've had shit relationships,' she says. 'I've always had shit from the male species. But Ashley is different, he is everything I could have wanted. He has ticked every box so I'm holding onto him with both hands.'

Hold on to him with both hands she did, and the pair shared nights in and evenings out together, including their first date, which saw them watching a gig by US soul supremo John Legend. Soon enough, Ashley had been given Cheryl's parents' seal of approval – despite playing football for a team that wasn't the Tweedy family's beloved Newcastle United. 'He makes me very happy and puts a big smile on my face,' she said, 'My mum really approves of him. Going out with an Arsenal player may not have been the best thing I could've done, but he plays for the country as well so that's fine. He gets away with it with my dad... just.' Their football rivalries didn't cause too many problems, with Cheryl insisting her loyalties still lay with the Toon. 'I'm a Newcastle fan and when they play Arsenal I sit in the black and white side,' she says. 'I hope we beat them – but I secretly hope Ashley's OK with it. I totally take the piss if we beat them and he does the same to me even if we're playing against someone else.'

Cheryl credited her new man with 'calming her down': 'When I met Ashley, it all changed and I don't argue with him. I feel a lot calmer. All my friends and family have said I became a different person when I met Ashley, although I haven't noticed it.'

The couple got engaged on a holiday in Dubai in June 2005, after eight months together and set a date for the wedding – 15 July 2006. 'When you find the right person, you know they are The One,' says Ashley. 'You just want to be with them forever. That's how it is with Cheryl. I don't want anyone else.' But it wasn't the first time a man had asked for Cheryl's hand in marriage; a young fan had proposed to her before Ashley. Cheryl explains, 'It's really flattering for anyone to go to those lengths, but sometimes it's just a bit scary.' Ashley's mum Sue was delighted by the engagement, albeit slightly confused when her son rang to tell her the news. 'I got a phone call from Ashley, who was in Dubai with Cheryl. And he said to me: "Mum, I've gone and bought a ring." And I thought, oh yes, that's nice, and then I realised what he meant and was like, "Have you asked her to marry you?" and he said, "Oh yeah, that's what I meant." I was so happy because Cheryl is such a lovely girl and they are so good together.'

Ashley had called Cheryl's dad Garry before he proposed, although like Sue before him, he was rather flummoxed by the conversation. 'I don't think he believed it was me at first – he thought it was a prank,' says Ashley. With the £50,000 sparkler on Cheryl's finger, the singer branded it the happiest day of her life, and admitted she couldn't wait to become a footballer's wife – and didn't mind the tabloid-given title of 'the new Posh and Becks'. 'I couldn't believe it when he popped the question but now I can't wait to be a footballer's wife. We'd joked about it but that was it. I was so shocked and he was crying. I'd never seen him cry before. It was honestly the happiest moment of my life. I didn't hesitate.' Cheryl knew Ashley was The One: 'He was everything I ever wanted in a relationship. It's like we're twins, like I'm hanging out with my best friend.'

The provisional date of summer 2006 for the wedding was a busy time – Ashley was playing for his country at the World Cup in Germany, while Cheryl was touring with the rest of the girls across the UK. But Ashley conceded he was letting his wife-to-be oversee the big day so she could organise the wedding exactly how she would want it to be. He said, 'I'm leaving the wedding plans to Cheryl. She can have whatever she wants. I want it to be the happiest day of her life, a day she will never forget.' And on 15 July 2006, Cheryl and Ashley shared their special day together with friends, family and Girls Aloud – and it certainly was a day to remember.

CHAPTER 14

2004: What Will the Neighbours Say?

FOR GIRLS ALOUD'S TV show pals, it was a good start to the year. Fellow *Popstars: The Rivals* contestants and newly-formed girl band Clea were on the verge of enjoying their second foray into the charts with 'Stuck In The Middle' – and reckoned they could 'do a Liberty X', forging a career out of their Popstars failure. Clea member Lynsey Brown said, 'The winners are meant to win and the losers were meant to lose. When I didn't make it into Girls Aloud, I thought my chance of a career might be over.'

Meanwhile, Girls Aloud were going from strength to strength. Cheryl began the new year on top form after the controversy over her assault of toilet attendant Sophie Amogbokpa in January 2003, playing to a sell-out crowd at Newcastle's Powerhouse, including her mum Joan. They enjoyed their time off over Christmas, and were looking to the year ahead. Nadine said, '(2003) has just been a rollercoaster the whole time. Until Christmas, we had no more than three days off in a row. We're not complaining. It's good to be busy – it's what we've wanted from the word go and it's been unbelievable.' Girl band stalwarts Atomic Kitten announced their split in January, leaving a void for Girls Aloud to fill. And fill it they would, with great gusto. But their fellow pop stars still continued to make derogatory comments about the band – little did they know 2004 would be the year Girls Aloud would have the UK eating out of their well-manicured hands.

Music journalists insisted 2004 would be the year pop would die out – because of a so-called 'rock revival', bands like Coldplay, The Darkness and Busted were spitting in the face of pop music and giving it a good old guitar-wielding thump. The last bastion of pop, and former Spice Girl Melanie C was still up to her Girls Aloud-dissing antics, branding the band 'pop puppets' She said, 'These people have to be puppets but it seems everyone is so expendable. Girls Aloud are doing really well but the Spice Girls was a global phenomenon. I don't think it is something that can be manufactured.' Lostprophets frontman Ian Watkins gave his verdict on the band, branding them 'brain-dead bimbos'. Girls Aloud took the singer's comments in their stride, and continued to work on their new album, which would shock – and impress – critics and fans alike.

Cheryl was faced with unwanted press interest when her brother Andrew made the headlines once again. He appeared in court in Newcastle over charges of breaking into a car and a separate incident where he swore at policemen. He was told by magistrates: 'You haven't got a blameless record and things are getting more serious. We will need to prepare reports before sentencing you but we are looking at punishments in the community band.' He was later sentenced to 150 hours community service and was fined £140 for being drunk and disorderly. Manager Louis Walsh told the press Cheryl was still deeply affected by the previous year's events, and that she wasn't eating properly four months after her conviction. 'Cheryl is still not over the whole thing,' he said. 'She's distraught and not eating. She is so wary of everyone.' But he insisted the experience had brought the girls closer together as a group. 'The other four totally support her. I think it has brought the band closer, even though there was a lot of negative publicity at the time. When you see someone so pretty crying in a lawyer's office, which I've seen her do twice, you feel really sorry for her, you worry for her.'

At the end of the month, the girls were off to Dublin for a charity gig at The Point Theatre, performing alongside Westlife, Rachel Stevens and Gareth Gates, among others. The girls couldn't wait for their second year at the Childline concert, and professed their love for Ireland's fair city. Kimberley said, 'We've had some brilliant times in Dublin. We always go out. The last time we did Childline all the bands went out together and it was a really good night, so I'm looking forward to it.' The group attended fellow Walsh protégée Samantha Mumba's 21st birthday in the city, letting their hair down and having a good time away from the pressures of the studio, where they were working on their second album. They partied their way through Dublin, and partied upon their return to London – so much so that Walsh decided to have a quiet word with the girls. According to reports, he said, 'I was called by two Polydor directors who both said they didn't want the girls turning up to the opening of an envelope.' He later said, 'They've learnt a hell of a lot since they started out. I don't care who they go out with as long as they do their jobs and don't let boyfriends get in the way. If they are happy they will work harder – and that will make me happy.'

With the band's love of all things Irish, the groups signed up to perform in both the North and South of Ireland during the St Patrick's Day celebrations on 17 March. What would appear to be an innocent celebration by anyone living across the Irish sea is in actual fact a contentious affair in Northern Ireland, thanks to years of politically charged fighting between the two main religious groups, Protestants and Catholics. Protestants see the celebration of the patron saint of Ireland as almost an exclusively Catholic affair.

Protestant politician Hugh Smith aired his disdain at the band performing at what he claimed was a segregated event. He said, 'Given the experience of recent years this is not what could be termed a cross community event. In fact, in view of the overt display of republican flag and emblems it would be virtually impossible for Protestants to participate. Some members of my wider family would be fans of Girls Aloud and I think the band has been very ill-advised to accept this invitation.' But Irene Sherry, the event's organiser, said, 'Anywhere in the world where St Patrick is celebrated there are going to be Tricolours (the green, white and gold flag of Ireland). This is an inclusive event and everyone is welcome. We hope to have 20-30,000 people coming along to enjoy a memorable experience with a number of bands including Girls Aloud.'

Love-wise, it was a tough time for the band. Nadine split from her long-term love Neil McCafferty, Kimberley and boyfriend Martin Pemberton called it a day, Sarah and Mikey Green were going through a 'trial separation' and Cheryl was desperately seeking a potential suitor. Sparks flew as Nadine was linked to footballer Matt Etheridge – the former boyfriend of Neil McCafferty's sister Claire. Newspapers alleged the singer had been dating the West Ham player, despite Etheridge and Claire having an eight-month old child together. 'This is a nightmare,' she said. 'The story is so untrue and it is hurting people for no reason. At the end of the day, when there is nothing going on, rumours and stories like this are just so frustrating.' Sarah's ex Mikey was linked with Hollywood A-listers Alicia Silverstone and Keira Knightley, but the couple soon rekindled their romance. A few weeks later in March, Nicola would be the final member of the band to split with her man – although her separation from childhood sweetheart Carl would prove to be short lived.

The girls were looking forward to their return to

Dublin for the St Patrick's Day celebrations, and were upset when the event had to be cancelled due to bad weather. High winds and rain had made the stage unsafe, and Irish fans were left disappointed at not seeing the girls perform. Their manager, Louis Walsh said, 'Everyone was really disappointed. They were all looking forward to coming over for Paddy's weekend. Girls Aloud are recording their new album at the minute and they are based in London, but everyone, especially Nadine, was really excited about coming to Ireland.' The let-down of not travelling to the south of Ireland was temporarily allayed when the girls travelled to Belfast to sing at the contentious St Patrick's Day concert outside the City Hall, sharing the stage with Shane MacGowan and *Fame Academy* stars Sinead Quinn and Malachi Cush. The band went down a treat during their first Northern Irish performance, and Nadine was delighted to be back in her home country. 'It's always great to be back home,' she said. 'I'd love to be in Derry too, but it's great to be in Belfast.' So great, in fact, Nadine returned to London with a heavier suitcase – several pairs of men's pants had found their way on stage during the band's performance, and the enterprising star lifted them for posterity. 'I ended up going home with five pairs of boxer shorts that fans had thrown,' she explained. 'I was dancing around on the stage and they started coming from all directions. It was a bit surreal.'

On their return to London, the girls were concentrating on the follow-up to *Sound Of The Underground* in the studio. After the release of the

Xenomania's reworking of the Pointer Sisters' 'Jump', rumours abounded a trade-off had been made between Girls Aloud bosses and the company's songwriting team to let them mastermind the entire second album. It was no secret Brian Higgins wasn't a fan of the cover track, but negotiated the deal to have his way on the new album if he complied with the record company's demands. This time, the girls would have an input into the songs, stamping their own seal on the forthcoming long-player. Cheryl explained, 'We've each written a track for the album. I've finished mine but the other girls are still recording theirs.' Kimberley added they were taking a new approach for their second album. 'The last time around I just remember feeling like I had no energy because we just sat around and ate all day,' she said. 'It was just pure boredom. It would be like, 'All right, meal time's finished, let's get another meal.' But this time we went to the gym every day in the morning and that kick-started us.' But Nadine worried that such a long gap between their last single release in November and their next, slated for June, would jeopardise their popularity: 'We really want to build up our fans again. We're scared we've lost our entire fan base and we're nervous about getting up on stage and no-one caring that we're there.'

Girls Aloud's fears were allayed when they were named as the headliners of a huge outdoor gig in Ireland. Nadine was overjoyed when she learned that the band had been signed for Radio 1's series of summer gigs in April, billed as One Big Weekend. This year, it was scheduled to take place in Derry – Nadine's much-loved home town. 'I have dreamed of this moment all my life. All my friends and family are going to be there which will make me very nervous.' But she added she couldn't wait to have Kimberley, Sarah, Nicola and Cheryl in the city. 'I'm going to treat all the girls to a big night out on the town in Derry and show them it's the best place in the world!' Back home, Nadine was given the ultimate freebie – a swish Mercedes by a local car dealership. She had just passed her driving test, and owner Bob Mullan thought it was about time the Derry girl-done-good deserved a treat. He said, 'We contacted her a couple of months ago and asked if she'd like a free car for a year. Nadine's a great girl. She's a real home-grown pop idol and deserved a treat.' Ironically, around the same time, Cheryl crashed her Toyota RAV4 motor, but luckily was unhurt.

But the excitement was to be short-lived, as the Derry girl soon fell victim to the frightening side of fame – and was being plagued by the wily antics of a stalker. She said, 'It's very creepy. He's been leaving me messages on my mobile. I've taken it very seriously. The person knows a lot about where I have been and what I've been doing. I'm so scared. I'd been in Lanzarote with my mum on holiday and one day I was walking along the sea shore and I got a text saying, "Did you enjoy your walk along the beach?" When I got home, I went out to my car but it wasn't in my parking space. It was in a different one and there were flowers under the wipers. And I was thinking, "Am I just freaking out or is this weird?" He still rings and just hangs up. But I've never reported it to the police.'

Cheryl hit the headlines in June – the nation was once again gripped by *Big Brother* fever, and so was Ms Tweedy. She wasn't too impressed with *Big Brother* contestant Michelle Bass' antics on the reality TV show, and wanted to make her opinion heard. Newcastle-born Michelle quickly gained a reputation for stripping off, shamelessly flirting with fellow contestant Stuart Wilson, he of the long luscious locks and 'hip' facial hair. Cheryl insisted Michelle was giving Geordies an unwelcome public representation. 'Michelle embarrasses me and the place where I was born, and she has given Geordies a bad name. When I heard there was going to be a girl from Newcastle in the house, I thought I would support her, but I realised after about three days that she was a complete idiot. Everything she does is for the cameras and the only reason she has made a play for Stuart is to help her win the show. Everyone in Newcastle will be hoping she gets voted out before she does anything else to make us look stupid.' Kimberley mounted the rumour mill during the same month, with tabloids claiming the singer's infamous pout wasn't at all what it seemed; they couldn't believe a girl could have such full lips without the aid of a cosmetic boost. At the end of the month, fresh from being named Band Of The Year by *Glamour* magazine, the girls once again took to the stage at London's G-A-Y to give fans a taster of their new tunes. Cheryl celebrated her 21st birthday on stage at the gig, where she was given a cake and serenaded by the audience, who sang a rousing rendition of 'Happy Birthday'. The Monday after, fifth single 'The Show' was released. The record-buying public would decide whether the band was deserved of its pop crown after a seven-month break from the charts.

All the stops had been pulled out for the video. 'The Show' was set in a beauty salon in a central London studio, with each of the five girls adopting alter egos; Cheryl was body hair-waxer Maxi Wax; Nadine was beautician Frenchie; Nicola was the girl with the spray gun, Chelsea Tanner; Sarah was hairdresser Supa Styla; and Kimberley was in charge of fictional salon Curls Allowed as The Boss. The video had a very Sixties feel, with a five-way split screen featuring the whole band while they manipulated unsuspecting men who had dropped into the salon for a treatment. It was a particularly enjoyable shoot for Sarah, who studied hairdressing at college in her hometown of Stockport. She said of the video, 'I've been abusing the men, killing their hair and everything else, which was good fun because I used to hairdress when I was younger. I've got a lot of friends in that area, which will be laughing themselves silly when they see that because that's what I was like at college – I just didn't care. I was just like "yeah, whatever"' The girls danced with brooms in the video, and pioneered the dancing with chairs move they rolled out for their live stage performances of the song. Each girl had a specially designated directors-style seat with their name on the back. Kimberley reckoned it was the best shoot the girls had done: 'I think that's the most fun we've ever had on a video!' she quipped. On the song's release, it hit number two in the charts – giving the girls an unbroken run of five top five single releases. They couldn't knock US R&B heart-throb Usher from the top spot, but Girls Aloud were delighted by their latest chart success. Despite 'The Show' being lauded as a pop masterpiece, famed music critic Paul Morley thundered. 'They've been bullied into submission,' he wrote, before launching into a scathing attack on the girls, criticising their 'overexposure', their 'blank eyes and forced smiles', and branded them 'lost souls adrift in a world of hits, shit and glitter.' But Girls Aloud didn't care what the critics had to say – they knew they were good and certainly not one-hit wonders. 'In the beginning we said to ourselves that we'd take every day as it came, but we never thought it would be a case of us doing the TV show and then that was it,' explains Nicola. 'It didn't enter our minds; it was more the public and critics who thought more about it. Because we knew it wasn't going to happen it wasn't an issue for us at all.' June also saw the end of Sarah's relationship with Mikey Green for the second time, but Sarah hoped she would end up with the singer in the future: 'What has been keeping me going is the thought that we might be able to sort out things eventually. With the way things are going, we're both really busy and it's hard to make time to see each other.'

Rumours abounded of a new incarnation of *Popstars: The Rivals* at the time. After the success of Girls Aloud and failure of One True Voice, the show bosses planned to bill the programme *Popstars: Boy Meets Girl* – producing a girl/boy duo to take on the charts. Talent stalwart Louis Walsh was lined up to be on the judging panel, along with former Spice Girl Mel B, presumably spurred on by her ex-bandmate Geri Halliwell's success on *Popstars: The Rivals* in 2002. The show was slated to hit screens in the spring of 2005, but by this time, pop impresario Simon Cowell's new talent show *The X Factor* had well and truly dwarfed the *Popstars* franchise after its TV debut at the close of 2004.

As befitting a top-notch pop band, the girls' diaries were packed full of gigs and events during the summer months. They would perform at countless outdoor festivals up and down the country, including *T4*'s Popbeach in Great Yarmouth, Live + Loud in Scotland, Party in The Park in Swansea and Summer XS in Nottingham to name a few. They had been lined up to headline another Derry date in August at a city festival, but the plug was pulled on the event over a lack of funding. In July, tragedy was to befall the Coyle family. Within ten days in July, the Coyles suffered two bereavements – Nadine's mum Lillian's sister passed away, and shortly after, Nadine's beloved grandfather and Lillian's father, John Kavanagh, died. Nadine had been very close to war veteran John, phoning him every week she had been in the *Popstars* house, and unsurprisingly, he was extremely proud of his granddaughter's success. Speaking in 2002, he said, 'We're very proud of Nadine. She's done really well. I watched every show and voted for her – a couple of times each week!' Hit badly by the tragedy, Nadine flew back to Derry to be with her family, and was given time off to grieve. Her father Niall said,

'My wife Lillian and all the family suffered two terrible losses within a week. Her sister died just last Monday and her 79-year-old father this Sunday past. Nadine was very close to her grandfather so it was a very hard time for her. It is difficult for all of us. Nadine came back the day her aunt passed away and hasn't decided when she will leave again.'

At the end of July, Girls Aloud performed in Gateshead alongside Natasha Bedingfield, Will Young and Busted as part of *Top Of The Pops Alfresco*, which saw the long-running music programme having its first outside broadcast in the show's 40-year history. They sang and danced their way through the show on Cheryl's hallowed home turf – and didn't care much that they had just been named the fourth worst dancers in pop by kids cable TV channel Trouble.

Trouble was the last thing on the band's mind after a shoot was forced to be abandoned when Nicola got into a bit of a scrape – or rather, a near-death experience. The *Mirror* reported Nadine had performed a rescue during a high-octane episode involving Nicola, an east London rooftop and a fashion shoot for a magazine. Nicola fainted in the sunshine after being dressed in winter attire, and was saved by Nadine, who reacted instantly to the unfolding drama. 'I don't remember what happened,' explains Nicola, 'It was all a bit of a blur. I was already feeling faint as we were wearing winter clothes and it was boiling hot weather. All I remember is getting my heel caught on the railings, then losing my balance and Nadine screaming as she caught me in her arms. Nadine and Kimberley pulled me away from the edge and all the girls sat me down and were worrying about me. It was terrifying. I couldn't stop shaking for a couple of hours.' Nadine added, 'One minute we were laughing and the next I could feel Nicola's arm slipping off my shoulder and saw her falling back. I just screamed and grabbed her arm. Once Nicola was safe and we calmed her down I couldn't stop thinking about what might have happened. It was scary.'

Nicola was given the once over by doctors due to her fainting spells, with the medics even suspecting she was suffering from an eating disorder after Girls Aloud bosses allegedly ordered the band to cut out junk food from their diets. 'I have always had a massive appetite. I never put on any weight but our management thought it was bad for my health so I was told to cut out the burgers and stuff completely. I felt really weak and sick all the time,' she explains. 'I just didn't have any energy and I was taken to a doctor for blood tests. He thought I was diabetic but I was just missing food. They even suspected I was bulimic but I was just trying to be healthy. They put me on iron tablets. It was an awful time – I was miserable because I was hungry.'

After the girls' busy summer schedule, it was time for their second release from the forthcoming second album. 'Love Machine' was a belter of a song. The video was shot at London club Titanic, giving the video a classic smoky jazz club feel – and made it look like a night out with the girls. Sarah said, 'It's got more of a timeless feel about it.' Nadine added, 'It reminds me of a

TV show back in the Fifties or something.' Kimberley in pink, Nadine in yellow, Sarah in white, Nicola in baby blue and Cheryl in green, shimmied their way around the renamed Eskimo Club setting, sipping champers, cavorting on tables, and dancing in formation, flanked by impressive laser-style lights and disco balls. On 13 September the song was released, charting at number two; it was kept off the top slot by popular dance tune 'Call On Me' by Eric Prydz, a reworking of Steve Winwood's 1982 hit 'Valerie', featuring scantily clad ladies doing a sexually-charged aerobics class in various shades of the rainbow. The song even led Scottish paper the *Daily Record* to brand the girls better than the most famous female five piece before them upon the release of 'Love Machine': 'Once upon a time Girls Aloud positioned themselves as the new Spice Girls, but it's doubtful whether Geri and Co would have had the clout to carry off such a striking pop tune. Wonderful.' The comparison was certainly warranted – with 'Love Machine' charting at number two, it made Girls Aloud the first girl group since the Spice Girls to score six top three hits in a row. Perhaps fuelled by Kimberley, Cheryl, Nicola, Sarah and Nadine's match of her old group's record, rumours emerged that Geri was battling Girls Aloud to land the coveted Children In Need song for 2004. Girls Aloud triumphed, and 'I'll Stand By You' was the official song for the annual BBC-organised event.

It was in October that reports linked Cheryl to Arsenal and England footballing ace Ashley Cole, and soon the pair began dating. The new romance helped keep the singer's mind off her brother Andrew, who was once again in trouble with the law for riding his motorbike without insurance and failed to stop for police who were in pursuit of the erstwhile Tweedy. He was given a £200 fine by Newcastle magistrates and awarded six points on his driving licence.

The girls' seventh single, 'I'll Stand By You' was a swift departure for the band. A Brian Higgins arrangement of the 1994 hit for The Pretenders, it was the group's first ballad. The accompanying video saw the girls on a deserted beach on a desert island – filmed in a studio, naturally – dressed in raggedy clothes and looking moody slumped against trees. Cheryl expressed her disdain at the sand 'going everywhere', and Nicola admitted it was a difficult shoot. 'It's always a lot easier to do a video for a faster song as you're dancing, smiling, you're having a laugh,' she explained. 'But when the video's like this you just feel so cheesy.' Faced with a stylist armed with a spray-tan, she joked, 'I don't do the sunkissed look – I do the red raw look.' Of the choice of song, Nadine said, 'The song is totally different for us as a band. Everybody knows the song so well. I hope Chrissie Hynde (The Pretenders' frontwoman) doesn't mind too much and that you're not going to make too much of a fool of yourself really.' Cheryl added, 'All of our songs have been uptempo and quite dancey, and we just wanted a really beautiful ballad that shows off all of our voices, and just to show a variety that we can actually sing a slow song – and that we can actually sing.' On its release, and bolstered by its official Children In Need single status, the group hit number one on 21 November, knocking U2 off their top of the chart perch, holding off a challenge from Destiny's Child, and managing to sell 58,000 copies in its first week of release. The song stayed there for two weeks before being usurped from the top spot by another charity offering, the star-studded 'Do They Know It's Christmas' by Band Aid 20.

What Will The Neighbours Say was released on 29 November to great acclaim, and the critics were falling over themselves to praise the second offering from Girls Aloud. Caroline Sullivan, writing in the *Guardian,* described the 14-track album in reverential terms – comparing it to a seminal 1978 release by pop/rock legends Blondie. 'The album plays in the background, sounding like a baby-punk version of Blondie's *Parallel Lines,'* she wrote. Another critic wrote with apparent disbelief at the oxymoron of Girls Aloud's music: 'They are the most manufactured of bands, yet completely original. Their songs are witty, exuberant and ground-breaking, built around sounds from all the files in the pop archive.'

While this time around the album was made by Xenomania in its entirety, the girls were on board to boost their songwriting credentials. 'A lot of people think we don't have credibility because we didn't write our own songs on the first album,' said Cheryl. But this time around, five tracks on *What Will The Neighbours Say?* were penned by the girls – 'Hear Me Out' (Sarah), 'Thank Me Daddy' (Kimberley), 'I Say A Prayer For You' (Nicola), '100 Different Ways' (Nadine) and 'Big

Brother' (Cheryl). Nadine said in 2003 she 'couldn't write a song': 'Some of the girls write their own songs. I don't think I could write my own stuff, but some of the girls are great at it.' Luckily, Xenomania supremo Brian Higgins coaxed Girls Aloud's collective songwriting ability out. He explains, 'We don't let them out of the room until they've given every ounce of melodic instinct that they've got in them... then we pile some more in. And when you listen back to the completed track at the end, you find they've contributed really well.' On the album was a song originally meant for US pop queen Britney Spears – who turned it down 'because it didn't have a chorus.' Higgins says, '[Britney's] record company loved it, but Britney's people said, "Where's the chorus? Why are there no repetitive parts?"' Thankfully, 'Grafitti My Soul' and its tales of spike-heels and skintight jeans remained in the hands of Girls Aloud, who delivered the song's three minutes and 15 seconds of slinky pop-rock to perfection. Higgins admitted that while he, Miranda Cooper and the rest of the Xenomania stable down in Kent wrote the songs, if they didn't 'fit' with Girls Aloud, then they were dropped. 'No matter how good a tune might be, if the girls couldn't take charge of it and get us excited, we'd chuck it out.' The *Daily Telegraph* branded *What Will The Neighbours Say?* 'a glorious piece of pop trash, with surprising hidden depths,' singing Girls Aloud's praises while leaving nothing but scathing words for their reality TV show-created contemporaries. The *Observer* music critic Kitty Empire was just as complimentary, opining '...that there might be some elusive, genre-transcending will-'o-the-wisp known as 'good' music and that Girls Aloud have managed to track it down and seize it.' The album charted at number six, selling 85,717 copies in its first week of release, and has since gone double platinum.

Critics also attributed their success to not only the girls' pop posturing, but believed another strength lay in their fashion sense. Stylist to the stars Kenny Ho was aboard the Girls Aloud clothes horse following a colourful career dressing the Spice Girls, David Bowie and Westlife, and transformed the girls' look. Journalists praised Ho's work with the fivesome, putting them in high-street threads – and styles easily copied by their fans, not unobtainable items such as Gucci trousers, Jimmy Choos or Louis Vuitton handbags; celebrity fashion must-haves aren't exactly in the price range of most.

The success of the new album and the critical acclaim Girls Aloud were garnering led to rumours the band was going to try to crack America in March 2005. The girls also announced details of their first ever tour, which was going to take place in May of the following year. Kimberley said, 'We've been itching to do this for a long time. But we decided to wait until we had two albums worth of songs to perform before we took to the stage. The time is right for us to give the fans a show they deserve. We're so excited!'

The close of the year saw the girls' most high profile performance to date – The Royal Variety Performance at the London Coliseum on 14 December. They sang 'The

Show' in front of a star-filled audience which included Prince Charles, Prince of Wales. 'The Royal Variety Performance for Prince Charles was just surreal,' explains Nicola. 'We went on at the end to sing the National Anthem and he was sitting in his little box, and there we were on the front row next to Elton John, Olivia Newton-John and Liza Minnelli. We were all elbowing each other down the line and laughing. I got lots of texts from my mum and my family saying, 'What were you laughing at?' but we just couldn't believe what we were doing. Backstage afterwards we had to wait in a line to meet the Prince, and I shook his hand and said, "Nice to meet you," and he said, "Well done."' But Nicola admits the heir to the throne wasn't top of her 'must-meet' list: 'To be honest, I wanted to meet Elton John more than Prince Charles. He came over and was saying how well he thought we were doing. When we got back to our dressing room, we just looked at each other and started screaming!'

In December, the band was linked to New Look, with the papers claiming Girls Aloud had signed a six-figure deal with the fashion chain to design clothes for 16-24 year olds, which would debut in New Look's Spring/Summer 05 collection. However, this proved not to be the case, as fashion retail industry bible *Drapers* unequivocally stated a week later that the claims were false and no deal had been signed between the two parties. Just before Christmas, Cheryl, Nicola, Nadine, Sarah and Kimberley visited Great Ormond Street Children's Hospital in London, to give out mp3 players to the children.

The girls were given a three-week break over the Christmas holidays, and each intended to enjoy it, spoil their friends and family, and reflect on their hectic year as pop's greatest hope since Blondie. Despite reports the girls had been given a £1 million Christmas bonus, Kimberley's mum Diane was quick to deny the allegations: 'It would be very nice, but no, I don't think they've had one.' But she added her daughter had got her some useful gifts for the festive season. 'She bought me a DVD recorder,' she said, 'which will be really useful for recording what she is doing, and a very nice handbag which would be too expensive for me. They are going to be busy in the New Year, but Kimberley is still loving it.' Nicola asked Santa for a car, as she had booked to do her driving test in the New Year. She said, 'I want a little Audi TT, which is such a girly car, and I want it in black with a red leather interior. So I'm just going to have to write that letter [to Father Christmas] and tell him how good we've been this year.'

Cheryl spent her festive season opening a few family football rivalries – her boyfriend Ashley Cole was playing on an Arsenal side facing Newcastle United. But Cheryl insisted she'd be cheering on the Toon, and not her beau. After the well earned break, Sarah, Nicola, Nadine, Kimberley and Cheryl braced themselves for what was going to be a busy year ahead.

CHAPTER 15

2005: Girls on the Road

GIRLS ALOUD STARTED the year with something of an inter-pop feud. With their 30-date What Will The Neighbours Say? Tour in the pipeline, it turned out that one of their gigs at the Aberdeen Exhibition and Conference Centre was billed for 13 May – the same night former judge and mentor of Popstars: The Rivals, Geri Halliwell, had wanted to perform. A spokesperson for the venue said the allocations were made on a 'first come, first served' basis, and that Girls Aloud had got there first. Over two years ago, would Geri have thought she would have been playing to similarly-sized crowds as her Popstars protégées? Probably not.

The excitement of the girls' first ever tour had captured the imaginations of the band and fans alike. More dates had to be added as tickets sold out within a matter of hours, with fans camping out to get their hands on tickets to see Kimberley, Nadine, Nicola, Sarah and Cheryl in the flesh. Girls Aloud couldn't quite believe their success so far, and even months after their second offering *What Will The Neighbours Say?* hit the shops, they were still in awe of what they had achieved in such a short space of time. 'If we weren't doing this we'd be working the checkout in Tesco,' opined Cheryl. 'We didn't have a chance to clock what we were doing. We were just catapulted into the middle of it all.' Sarah added, 'Hardly anybody out of reality TV gets to make a second album, so it had to be shit hot. I think it is fucking brilliant if I'm honest.' Kimberley had her own ideas explaining Girls Aloud's appeal: 'I think what people like about us is that we haven't had media training. They can see our mistakes.'

But before the tour was to begin in May, Girls Aloud had their diaries packed to the brim with social engagements and an endless stream of rehearsals and public appearances. Nadine became an agony aunt for the day on the pages of *Glamour* magazine, suggesting spurned lovers should 'go to his place and trash' the homes' of philandering men, while the band as a whole visited Bluecoat School in Oldham as part of a Radio One competition – spending the day doing maths lessons and playing an impromptu game of netball. Nicola's love of student culinary favourite, the Pot Noodle, was exposed by the *Guardian*, which regaled readers of her request for the cup-based snack in lieu of a fancy buffet. 'Chicken and mushroom please. The green one!' she is reported as saying to someone sent out to procure the item.

Cheryl's romance with footballer Ashley Cole was a

major source of interest for the tabloids, who speculated the pair was on the verge of getting engaged. Cheryl was certainly smitten, but admitted she understood the attention celebrity pairings merited. 'I've never been in a relationship like this where I've been treated like a princess,' she gushed. 'Maybe it's because I was much younger before, but it's more likely I kept picking idiot boyfriends. People will always have an opinion about our relationship. It's like when I heard about Charles and Camilla getting married. It's a weird one, because I really loved Diana. But I mean, if he's happy and he loves her, then so be it.' At a party thrown by US R&B star Usher in London, Cheryl told a journalist: 'We've spoken about marriage and are comfortable with it.' Naturally, the rumour mill went into overdrive, with a constant eye on the Geordie's left hand for the foreseeable future. Cheryl also hinted she was after a pooch to complete her new London-based family. She said, 'I have dogs at home which my mum looks after, but I really miss them. So I asked Ashley if we could get some but he didn't seem keen.' All was going well for the couple, although a move to Real Madrid was mooted after Ashley was fined £100,000 after illegally conducting talks with rival London side Chelsea. But Cheryl said, 'If I have anything to do with it, he'll be staying exactly where he is.'

At the end of the month, the girls once again travelled to Dublin to headline the Cheerios Childline charity gig – but ruffled a few feathers when Nadine refused to have her photo taken, thanks to a cold sore which had selfishly manifested itself on her face. Regardless of the facial flaws, Girls Aloud took to the stage and performed alongside acts such as Westlife and Lemar. Unlike the girls visit to Dublin almost a year ago to the day, they were on their best behaviour, and Nadine even confessed to have given up partying. 'I haven't been out partying for ages because it really gets to me,' she confessed. 'I get tired for about three days after and we're always performing these days. I've realised that you can't do everything – so now I go back to my apartment and put my pyjamas on.'

Their hectic schedule was taking its toll on the band, but Kimberley insisted all the hard work over the past two years was worth it. 'I can't get my head around the fact that we're doing better and better. I just can't believe we've managed to keep the momentum going. It can sometimes feel like being on a conveyor belt, and when it's like our 10th *GMTV* appearance and we have to be up at 4am, you could start to think, 'Why do we need to bother with this?' But I feel grateful they want to hear another song and I'm quite happy to get up at 4am if that's what it takes. I know there's millions of girls who would love to be where we are right now.'

February saw the girls adopt a series of sexy poses for men's magazine *Arena,* with the publication producing five different covers featuring each of the girls individually – *FHM* had done a similar thing towards the close of 2004. Serial singleton Sarah took the opportunity to plead with the well-placed folk at *Arena* to set her up with a man, saying, 'Can you lot find me someone? He could be a binman for all I care. It's personality that counts.' But behind the obvious physical beauty of the fivesome, Arena writer Chris Mooney admitted he was genuinely impressed with Girls Aloud's pop credentials. 'Arena couldn't dig up a single decent slagging off from anywhere,' he wrote. 'For the first time, reality TV has actually produced a pop group worthy of the name,' before launching into 'the ten reasons why Girls Aloud are the greatest group in the UK'. Girls Aloud would learn, over the next 12 months, that such high praise wouldn't come in fits and starts – by the time they unveiled their third long player in the Autumn, high-brow and esteemed music journalists were falling over themselves to lavish praise on the five former 'pop puppets' done good.

Girls Aloud were up for the Best Pop Act at the annual Brit Awards, sharing their category with Avril Lavigne, Natasha Bedingfield, McFly and Westlife. Sadly, the band lost out to the heirs to Busted's crown (Busted had split up the previous month), McFly. It wasn't the only setback for the Girls Aloud camp, as Cheryl discovered her brother Andrew's girlfriend had suffered a miscarriage. Youngest Tweedy sibling Garry said, 'Andrew's girlfriend was expecting a baby girl but she had a miscarriage. She was quite a long way into the pregnancy so it was devastating for her and Andrew. The whole family has been affected by this.'

Weeks later, Sarah suffered something of a fashion faux-pas at the Elle Style Awards in east London – and managed to rack up additional column inches through her proximity during proceedings to *T4* presenter Steve Jones. Her dress came undone at the back, giving the paparazzi an eyeful of her underwear. 'I'm so, so embarrassed,' she said. 'The buttons had come undone and I hadn't realised. I was wondering why all the photographers were shouting for me more than normal. This is awful. I was feeling really glamorous in the dress and now I can't even bear to think about what happened.'

Another performance at London club G-A-Y went down a storm on the verge of the release of new single 'Wake Me Up" despite Nadine being absent from the Girls Aloud line-up that evening. She had taken ill, and was recuperating while her bandmates belted out their tunes to the crowd. Earlier in the month, Sarah had been poorly and was forced to pull out of the National Hockey League (NHL) party at London's Hippodrome; and both absences led to rumours that all was not well in the Girls Aloud camp. Sarah was rumoured to have quit the band after a post on the website of producers Absolute – who have also worked with Will Young – revealed they would be working with the star. But Sarah was he was quick to respond saying, 'If anyone thinks I'm leaving, they're crazy. They're my girls and we're sticking together.' With Sarah still firmly on board, Girls Aloud got ready for 'Wake Me Up' to hit the charts.

The band's eighth single was released on 21 February, the fourth song to be taken from *What Will The Neighbours Say?* – and brought a feigned media outcry in its wake. The hoopla centred on the band's booze-referencing lyrics, which critics believed could influence young fans. However, passing mentions of margaritas and bottles of branded beer did nothing to keep the record-buyers at bay, and the song charted at number four – making it Girls Aloud's record-breaking eighth consecutive top five hit. The *Sun* described the song as 'The five girls at their very best. A solid, full-on, raw and ready pop groove which is gradually helping put this bunch alongside the Spice Girls in the pop history books.'

The accompanying video helped to arouse more interest in the band, with Kimberley, Nicola, Nadine, Sarah and Cheryl atop the kind of motorbikes more commonly seen beneath the hirsute legs of hard-nosed bikers. The girls cavorted in revealing costumes on their mean machines, licking and sticking fake tattoos on their arms, and applying nail varnish while supposedly out on the open road. The almost theatrical dance routine employed enthusiastic head-shaking from the band, and hard-as-nails moves; before once again mounting their bikes and riding off into the studio's sunset backdrop. A performance on *Top Of The Pops* saw the girls recreate strands of the video, only this time with gravity-defying hair and a gaggle of screaming fans.

From two wheels to four wheels, Nicola celebrated their chart success by passing her driving test – despite Kimberley confessing months earlier she would be afraid if her bandmate ever got behind the wheel of a car. 'She's got no concentration span,' Kimberley explained, 'I'd worry myself sick if she had her driving test.' Undeterred, Nicola splashed out on the swanky Audi TT she had asked Santa for in December. While the girls were out spending admits rumours of a financial reward for their hard work since being formed in 2002, Cheryl expressed interest in opening a tanning salon up north. She said, 'I've paid off my mum's mortgage but I really want to buy a tanning salon. It will be a great little family-run business and we will call it Tweedy's Tanning.'

Expanding her career didn't end there for Cheryl, and she made a guest appearance as a presenter on ITV music show *CD:UK*. Being on the other side of the proverbial fence of performance scared Cheryl, but she managed to cope, spurred on by co-host Dave Berry. She said, '*CD:UK* went well but to be honest I was absolutely shitting myself. I enjoyed it but people don't realise how hard it actually is. I'm not saying I'd never do it again but I wouldn't look for a career in it.'

After over two years exclusively under the charge of Louis Walsh, the band drafted in a new co-manager to help mastermind the next chapters of their pop takeover. Hilary Shaw of Shaw Thing Management was taken on board as an additional manager for Girls Aloud – and she was well placed to fill the role. She had previously managed another girl group success story in the shape of 1980s legends, Bananarama. Rumours suggested Louis was not impressed by the band's new signing, and that Shaw's appointment was part of a bigger plan to sack him as the group's manager. But

Louis was keen to make the truth known. 'It was me who hired Hilary,' he fumed. 'She's not taking over management of the band. Hilary has been looking after the day-to-day running of the group because I can't be there all the time. We are working on exciting projects and there's no way they are going to sack me as their boss. I'm running the ship and the girls all know that. I haven't offended the girls. We have very open discussions about the future of the band and we know where we stand. The girls are happy with the direction the group is taking and if they had a problem, they would come to me direct.'

Louis also managed to add fuel by the bucketload to reports Nadine was leaving the band. 'I am going to manage Nadine as a solo star in a few years, but Girls Aloud have two albums left in them. I've never made it a secret that I would like to manage Nadine one day. She is one of the most talented girls I have ever worked with.' Despite Louis' promises the band still had contractual obligations to fill after only two albums, the rumours of Nadine's departure from Girls Aloud reached pandemic proportions. Nadine, however, had other ideas. 'I have no intention of leaving the girls and going solo,' she said. 'What sane person is actually going to want to leave the biggest girl band in the country? The story was rubbish.' Cheryl added, 'We are working incredibly hard and nobody is leaving the band. Although we've been going for over two years we feel like we are just starting out.' She added that the greatest hits album in the pipeline wasn't an indication Girls

Aloud was to split – despite the majority of compilation albums spelling the end for pop acts. She said, 'We're doing a greatest hits because we'll have had three albums – it's a natural thing. That doesn't mark the end of the band. Because we've had split rumours right from the start, they are like water off a duck's back.' The *Sun*'s Bizarre stalwart Victoria Newton was having none of it, and aired her tuppence worth in her daily showbiz pages: 'From the looks of things, I can't see their careers stretching beyond next year.' How wrong could she be? The readers of *FHM* certainly hoped the girls wouldn't slip away without trace – all five girls ranked in the sexiest 100 women in the world. Cheryl came in at number two, just behind Kelly Brook; Sarah was at number eight; Nadine, number thirty-five; Kimberley, number forty-four; and Nicola, number seventy-seven.

Rehearsals for the band's first tour were in full swing, and the girls couldn't wait to get on the road after nearly two and a half years without a proper touring experience. 'I genuinely don't think we were ready to tour before now. We have two albums of good material now so it's all worked out really well,' explained Cheryl. 'If a band tours after their first album, people know maybe the first two or three singles they've had out and that's all for the whole hour. It's not that entertaining because people don't know enough of their music. It's better for us to do it now – we know we're ready and confident about the tour.'

Before the tour even began, the girls were causing controversy. Brighton voting fans in the 2005 general election were unable to watch the count because the Brighton Centre had been booked by the band months before – according to election officials, no other area would be big enough for the task in hand. So for one night only, Girls Aloud transcended politics and replaced democracy with their own brand of what journalist and critic Julie Burchill dubbed 'pantyliner punk'.

The tour kicked off in Rhyl, Wales, to great acclaim. The girls sang and shimmied their way through the 15-track, four costume change set at 25 venues to over 70,000 fans, opening with the almost-so-good-it's-dangerous aural assault that is 'The Show'. Girls Aloud had some surprises up their sleeves, dressing up in school uniforms for a cover of Wheatus' 'Teenage Dirtbag' midway through the set. Sarah later said, 'We all change when we get on stage – we get quite lairy.' Unsurprisingly, the fans didn't seem to mind the band's ballsy demeanour. They closed with 'Sound Of The Underground', leaving gig-goers with a reminder of just how far they had come from their *Popstars: The Rivals* days. Sarah admits, 'The first night was so overwhelming. All of us were nearly in tears. We were like, finally, this is it, this is what we've been waiting for.' Cheryl agreed. 'I love touring,' she says. 'That was amazing, seeing the people that have made you who you are really, bought your albums, supported you the whole way through and you're giving them something back – you're bouncing off each other. I have days when I'm on the stage and there's thousands of people and you get this feeling come over you like "Oh my God, everybody in this crowd knows who I am, they're singing the songs we sing."' 'When you see the reaction of the people who are genuinely really into the band and into the music and to us as individuals, it is unbelievable,' says Nadine.

The set list for *What Will The Neighbours Say?* Live was as follows:

'The Show'
'Here We Go'
'Girls On Film'
'No Good Advice'
'Graffiti My Soul'
'Teenage Dirtbag' (originally performed by Wheatus)
'Wake Me Up'
'Life Got Cold'
'Deadlines And Diets'
'I'll Stand By You'
'Love Machine'
'Real Life'
'Girls Allowed' – with Le Freak (originally performed by Chic) interlude
'Jump'
'Sound Of The Underground'

Music journalists couldn't wait to give their verdict on the UK's best loved girl band's first tour. The *Guardian*'s Alexis Petridis opined, 'It is hard to think of another manufactured pop act so universally loved. There is something shambolic and very British about Girls Aloud live, a whiff of [1970s televised variety show] *Seaside*

Special adds to their idiosyncratic charm. Girls Aloud are a unique and delightful phenomenon.' While the *Daily Telegraph*'s review was slightly more scathing, it conceded the gig was 'like a day out in Blackpool – impossible not to enjoy'. London's *Evening Standard* described the audience as a mix of 'sparkly teenage girls with fake tans, young gay men with tight t-shirts and spiky hair, and a few randy young lads all geared up for a night of beer-fuelled leering', proof of the girls' universal appeal.

The variation in the Girls Aloud fan demographic wasn't lost on Nicola, who spied the eclectic mix of gig-goers from the safety of the various stages, night after night: 'I couldn't believe some of the faces in the audience,' she noted. 'There were punks in the front row, and gangs of 15-year-old lads at the back. A lot of our younger fans were there with their parents and they seemed to enjoy it too.' Kimberley added, 'Lots of guys come to our shows just to perv over us. It's true – they line up around the block for tickets. The girls who come to our shows really listen to the music and sing along, but the guys kind of just stand there and stare.'

The tour wasn't without minor dramatics. Nadine erroneously asked Brighton fans, 'How you feeling out there Nottingham?', while in Liverpool, they found themselves at the centre of a gun n' drugs heist. Police arrested two men at the city's posh Radisson SAS hotel where Girls Aloud were staying, seizing two kilogrammes of cocaine and £20,000 in cash. Sarah said, 'It was terrifying. There were police everywhere. We didn't know what was going on because there were so many police around.' Cheryl had some tour battle scars to share – but admitted they hadn't affected her enjoyment of the live performance. She explained, 'It's been fantastic – we haven't had too many hiccups. I got punched in the eye backstage on the first night in the hustle and bustle but that's all. The tour has been an experience.' So said all of the girls. 'It's nice to spend a whole month performing and singing every night, dancing and you know, just that atmosphere that you get from a live show that you don't really get from anything else. It just felt like, this is what it's all about, really,' said Kimberley after the tour was over. Nicola added, 'I just had the best time of my life on that tour. Just without a shadow of a doubt, from the minute it started in rehearsals when we met the boys and were doing the dancing until the night it ended.' A DVD of *What Will The Neighbours Say? Live* was later released in November 2006, five months after their debut DVD *Girls On Film* – featuring the girls' music videos to date and TV performances – hit the shops.

The mobile Girls Aloud party ground to a halt in Dublin, the last night of the *What Will The Neighbours Say?* Circus, and after the last note of 'Sound Of The Underground' rang out, Kimberley, Sarah, Nadine, Cheryl and Nicola let their collective hair down at the city's swish club Lillies Bordello. Despite the band's success on their inaugural tour, rumours still managed to perpetuate about a split – and this time it was Cheryl on the way out. 'I'm not walking out on the

n 2006, Girls Aloud performed live in front of over 150,000 fans on their hemistry tour. They also fitted in shows at *(above)* an England vs New ealand rugby match, *(below left)* that summer's V Festival and smaller enues like the Pavilion Theatre in Rhyl, Wales *(below right)*.

Above: After overcoming her nerves before her first gig in hometown Derry, Nadine now loves to sing in front of an Irish crowd. Here she is with Sarah a an outdoor festival in Dublin, 2004.

Below: Nicola with Sarah and Nadine at the Kent Music Festival, 2005.

Above: At the Chelmsford leg of 2006's V Festival.

Below: Cheryl and Sarah in their element, singing and dancing in front of a live audience.

Above: Nicola with boyfriend Carl Davis.

Below left: Nadine with former beau Jessie Metcalfe at the height of their romance.

Below right: Cheryl with husband Ashley Cole.

Watch out, the paparazzi's about!

Above left: Nicola leaving the CD:UK studios.

Above right: Sarah at an aftershow party.

Below left: Cheryl is caught popping out for some fish and chips while back home in Newcastle.

Below right: Nadine signs autographs for fans after a TV appearance.

The girls have used their high profile to publicise good causes, including Comic Relief and the Variety Club. They collaborated with the Sugababes in March 2007 on the charity single 'Walk This Way' (*top*, with comedian Russell Brand) and launched the Gold Heart Appeal at Harrods.

Above: Girls Aloud are style icons for millions of girls up and down the country. Their own Barbie range has outfits designed by the girls, inspired by favourite items from each of their wardrobes.

Below: Curls Aloud! Promoting Sunsilk haircare products in April 2007.

Beautiful, talented and at the top of their game, Nadine, Kimberley, Cheryl. Nicola and Sarah have unmistakably changed the pop music landscape forever.

girls,' she insisted. 'Every few weeks someone says one of us is going to leave.' Cheryl was adamant she wasn't going to 'Do a Geri' and leave the UK's best girl band at the height of their fame, as the lady known as Ginger Spice had done several years before. Girls Aloud told journalists they didn't want to be as big as the founding fathers – or rather mothers – of Girl Power and attempt to crack America, despite reports to the contrary. 'I just think it's unrealistic,' said Nadine. 'I believe that if you want to break America you need to be there for six to eight months. But we're not really willing to let go of how big we are in Britain and Europe. We've been over there to do some recording in LA and all that, but we're not going to try to break ourselves over there.' Sarah explained, 'The Spice Girls were the first ones to do it in that respect on that scale. But it's difficult to achieve something like that twice in a row. I suppose we would have loved that level of success. But it would probably have killed us – so maybe it's just as well we never got it!'

The girls had a well-deserved break after the gruelling tour, landing a reported £250,000 deal to become the spokesmodels for haircare range NU:U, which shared the same parent company, Jemella, as ubiquitous straightening iron manufacturer GHD. With the Sexiest Soccer Babe accolade now under her belt (as voted for by readers of *FHM*), Cheryl headed for a relaxing holiday in Dubai with Ashley. After months of wedding rumours, Ashley finally popped the question with a £50,000 engagement ring. The pair soon returned to the

UK, where the couple's friends and family were looking forward to congratulating the future Mr and Mrs Cole. Kimberley and her beau Justin headed to Egypt, where Justin unfortunately fell victim to a bout of the mumps. But Cheryl's good news was tinged with sadness; her troubled brother Andrew was to be jailed for four years for his part in a mugging, and would undoubtedly miss the couple's wedding. At the time, Cheryl insisted her nuptials would not be a magazine-sponsored affair, saying, 'We're not going to do a mag deal. We just want it to be a quiet affair with everyone we love there. I've decided I'm going to give a wedding picture to everyone as a thank you for all the support I've had.'

It soon transpired that despite her new status as a taken woman, Cheryl was attracting attention from the most unlikely of sources, namely Pamela Anderson's ex, Mötley Crüe drummer Tommy Lee. His manager said, 'We tried to invite them to a party. Vince [Neil, the band's singer] said, "Dude, you've got to invite a band called Girls Aloud". Lee insisted, 'We've got to, dude. Fuck she's hot. Cheryl Tweedy. Fuck. She's amazing looking. Cheryl Tweedy... she is fucking amazing. She just got engaged? Dammit.' From love to the other side of the coin, hate, and to Charlotte Church. Upon hearing the opera-singer-turned-popstrel's breakout single 'Crazy Chick', Cheryl accused Charlotte of 'using Girls Aloud's old sound', thus igniting a long-running and vicious war of words between the pair.

In July, it was revealed that Cheryl and Ashley were being targeted by a gang of thieves who were allegedly plotting to rob the couple and steal the singer's £50,000 engagement ring. Cheryl said, 'The whole thing has been pretty scary, I don't really know what is going on and neither does Ashley. It's scary. I'm not wearing my ring.' After the furore died down and the pair were under the relative safety of police surveillance, Cheryl was back on form, and had devised a plan to deal with the wily would-be pilferers should she ever come face to face with them. She quipped, 'I would have slapped [the robbers] in the face with my shoes. They're scum, picking on a young girl.'

The summer months were a time of new beginnings for Girls Aloud. While they juggled working on their new album with spells at summer concerts and festivals throughout the country, new puppies were brought into the Girls Aloud world. Despite not seeming too enamoured with the idea of a pooch, Ashley caved in and bought Cheryl a Chihuahua named Buster. Not one to be outdone, Nadine was given a Yorkshire terrier pup from her parents for her 20th birthday – but couldn't decide on a name for the pet. Dad Niall explained, 'She was tied between calling it Vegas or Derry. But a good friend of ours has a daughter called Derry and Nadine thought it might not look too good to turn around and call the dog Derry.' Vegas it was, then.

Another established pop name had a go at Girls Aloud, despite the girls almost entirely having shaken off their reality TV mantle. Phil Oakey of Eighties electro legends Human League was up in arms over the band's success, and dubbed them as merely 'something off Page Three'.

'I'm glad we grew up at that particular musical time,' he says. 'Look around now and it's bloody Girls Aloud. I'm not here to knock them, but the fact is that they are a bunch of Page Three girls who release songs, not for musical reasons, but as souvenirs – as another form of merchandise. It's more important for them to stay in the gossip pages of the tabloids than produce music.'

But in the meantime, the girls had a single to release. 'Long Hot Summer' was the first single off the as yet untitled Girls Aloud third album, and it was set to go down a storm. Its rock-tinged pop hook with a cheeky side order of rap was expected to fly up the charts, not least because of its raunchy video, filmed at a garage on the outskirts of London. Girls Aloud in boiler-suit shocker! Kimberley, Nadine, Cheryl, Nicola and Sarah were clad in navy jumpsuits at GA Autos for the video – but naturally, for the girls, the all-in-ones were teamed with spangly heels and jewellery in a nice juxtaposition. A minute into the video, the girls remove their overalls, abandon the myriad car parts, their calendar of muscle-bound men and their collection of mini fans and get down to a bit of fancy choreographed dancing. After its release on 22 August, 'Long Hot Summer' became the first Girls Aloud song not to chart in the top five – it came in at a respectable number seven, despite only selling a disappointing 18,541 copies. The top ten that week was filled with easy-listening acts such as James Blunt, Daniel Powter and Simon Webbe – it seemed as if the girls' pop fanbase had fled the country and left the chart in a state of anarchy.

September saw Sarah don her party frock and perform bridesmaid duties at the wedding of Katie Price, AKA Jordan, and her beau, 1990s pop hunk Peter Andre at Highclere Castle in Hampshire. She would join ex-Atomic Kitten star Kerry Katona and Liberty X member Michelle Heaton as bridesmaids for the glamour girl at the celebrity wedding of the year. The pair were good pals – with Sarah thanking their 'tomboyish demeanour' for their common bond. 'I can be a bit tomboyish,' she says, 'But that's because I have a warped sense of humour – that's why Katie and I get on so well. She's hilarious! In a way we're both ladettes, but we don't look like tomboys. People might look at us and think, butter wouldn't melt, and then we open our mouths and they're like, "Bloody hell!"'

Later that month, Cheryl travelled to Newcastle to launch Marks & Spencer's Per Una lingerie collection at the city's Northumberland Street store. She revealed she was planning a shopping spree with fellow footballer's wife Victoria Beckham – not, sadly, in Marks & Spencer, but in Madrid – after a fashion faux pas on her entry to the WAGs' inner sanctum. 'The first time I went to an England match to watch Ashley was so embarrassing,' she explains. 'All the other girls were really glammed up, then I walked in with chipped nail polish and wearing a jumper. I think I looked terrible. But Victoria was down to earth and welcoming. She's going to take me shopping in Madrid. I'd love her to style me because she always looks fantastic. I don't know how she does it with three young sons. I really look up to her.'

In October, it was revealed that plans were afoot to do the unthinkable – release two singles and an album within just four weeks of each other. 'Biology' would be Girls Aloud's rooty-toot-toot back into the charts, while 'See The Day' was at the other end of the musical spectrum – cool, calm, collected, and a cover of Dee C. Lee's 1985 hit. Colin Barlow, joint managing director of the girls' record label Polydor, said it was a move to harness both ends of the Girls Aloud spectrum. 'We looked at the group's fanbase, which is incredibly broad, and we thought if we could get two singles out there that cater for both sides of the audience, it would drive people to the album,' he says. 'We're leading with the uptempo track but the ballad will follow quickly after.' The girls admitted the new album would be something of a musical departure from their previous offerings. Cheryl had said of the album earlier in the year, 'We're going to experiment a bit this time but we're definitely not going to rush this album through. We want to have more of our own input on this one. It's more of a stamp on our songs when we have our own input. But to be honest, we leave a lot of it to the professionals as well. We're not that experienced yet.'

An interview with gay men's magazine *AXM* saw the girls lose their feminine charm and become masculine for the day. Cheryl and Sarah were put in dungarees, Nadine was given a quiff, and collectively, the five were butched up for the accompanying photoshoot. During the interview, the girls spoke of their love for their gay fans, admitting they changed 'Long Hot Summer's reference to London's Old Kent Road in favour of Soho's Old Compton Street, London's most famous gay thoroughfare, for their army of gay fans during a performance at G-A-Y. Asked if they minded that gay women would be buying the magazine that month, Kimberley responded, 'Straight men get paranoid – "Oh my God a gay man fancies me." We don't. Girls can fancy us all day long.'

The feud between Charlotte Church and Cheryl exacerbated towards the end of the year. Charlotte had told a journalist, 'I'm like, love, you and me, singing competition, all right. That'd be brilliant – Geordie cow.' Cheryl hit back alleging Church was all talk and no trousers. 'Do you know what,' she told *AXM*, 'She's doing it all for publicity and the biggest joke of all is she shouted "hi ya" from one end of the corridor to the next when I last saw her. So she's not as hard to your face. We'd have a lot more respect for her if she ignored us, but the fact that she said "hi ya" in such a sweet fashion – it just made us think – "you fucking idiot."' More controversy was stirred, but this time about TV talent show *The X Factor*. Girls Aloud were accused of criticising the crop of wannabes trying out for fame, and as a result, were invited by judge Simon Cowell to sing live on the show, and invitation they declined as they insisted they hadn't been bad-mouthing the contestants.

The same month, it was announced that Girls Aloud were going into partnership with that famously dedicated follower of fashion, Barbie. Five dolls would be made as part of maker Mattel's Barbie Fashion Fever range, and would hit the shops in time for Christmas, aimed at six to seven–year–olds. A spokesperson for Mattel said the collaboration would 'reinforce Barbie's cool factor', through her restyle by the band. The band each designed a doll in their own image – Nadine's in a white dress and furry cardigan, Nicola's in white cropped trousers and a black top, Sarah, in a military-style jacket and trousers, Cheryl's in a white jacket, cropped top and black jeans, and Kimberley in a boho skirt and top. They were all different, but essentially the same – the central product was a Barbie at heart. But Kimberley noted the dolls weren't supposed to be clones of Girls Aloud. 'They haven't got the same faces,' she said, 'But they're not our exact faces... they're not like Madame Tussauds standard!'

Girls Aloud were delighted with the end result, not least because it conjured up fond childhood memories. Nicola said, 'We all remember playing with Barbie dolls. I forgot how much fun it is to dress her up in cool clothes – she's the ultimate girl's girl.' Bandmate Sarah added, 'We've had loads of fun giving Barbie a Girls Aloud makeover. The looks we've created are very now and we hope everyone loves them as much as we do.' Cheryl, however, expressed her jealousy over her five inch replica during an interview with *AXM*: '[To the doll] You bitch. It's too bloody good looking.' Nicola interjected with some comedy gold, saying, 'You should take it to the plastic surgeon.' Despite Cheryl's jealousy, her Barbie-based likeness sold out in the North East by the end of November, with disappointed fans having to be turned away from toy shops, such was her popularity on her home turf. In January 2006, the girls even made the cover of the official Barbie magazine – as their plastic alter-egos of course.

'Biology' was released on 14 November, and went straight in at number four. Industry bible *Music Week* dubbed it 'a strong step forward for Girls Aloud. A catchy, fresh sound that harks back to Eighties-era girl groups.' The girls' 10th single matched the Spice Girls' record of ten consecutive singles charting in the top ten. They were now on a par with their spiritual pop big sisters. Just before the release, Sarah collapsed after a performance on *CD:UK* due to a kidney infection, but soon recovered. The video saw the girls in a simple but stylish video, against three different backdrops and slowly-panning cameras. It opened with the band dressed in evening wear, in a posh setting complete with grand piano, chandeliers and matching candelabra, before the girls' outfits morphed into frilly pink and purple dresses against a different backdrop, reflecting the song's constant change of tempo. The third and final setting was a striking pink wallpaper with black embellishment, with the band clad in black, with red waist-cinching belts. Cue lots of jerky dancing, and it was a visual match made in heaven for 'Biology'.

After five months of hard work, so-called 'concept album' *Chemistry* was released on 5 December. The girls were excited by the prospect of their third album in three years, even admitting they listened to their own work. Girls Aloud knew they were getting better with age, and the humbling effect of still being popular long after their supposed sell-by date was not lost on the band. Cheryl said, 'A lot of pop acts make a big splash with their first album and then fade away. We've done things the other way round. Our albums have got better. If we weren't here, people would be crying out for a group like us.' As for the album itself, it was a genre-defining piece of pop history. Kimberley explained, 'There's definitely songs on there with completely different sounds that have never been heard before, which we always try to do.' These different sounds included the girls getting to grips with rapping on 'Watch Me Go' – something the band pulled off extremely well; there was no Madonna-style backlash similar to the furore which erupted after the Queen of Pop's foray into the spoken word on single 'American Life' in 2003.

Nadine certainly had high hopes for their third offering. 'We as a band want to take over the world. We want to do everything. We don't want to stop at the third album. We want this to go multi multi multi platinum.' With the sound of Ms Coyle's battle cries ringing in their ears, Girls Aloud hit the album chart at number 11 in a difficult week in the run up to Christmas – selling 81,962 in its first week would have almost guaranteed a number on album earlier in the year. Also released that week was a special limited edition of *Chemistry*, with an eight-track CD of Christmas tunes – both covers and new songs – and what was billed as 'a changeable Christmas sleeve'; rather than the simple portrait of the girls on the standard release, Sarah, Nicola, Nadine, Kimberley and Cheryl appeared as part of a festive vignette in 1950s style kitchen – Kimberley dressing the tree, Nadine complete with turkey, Cheryl and Nicola pulling an oversized cracker, and Sarah sampling the delights of some baked goods.

The album wasn't without its share of media-stirred controversy. The press expressed outrage over the allegedly saucy lyrics, and the first release from Girls Aloud to feature a swearword – Nadine utters the profanity 'shit' in 'Models'; a version of 'No Good Advice' had been recorded with the inclusion of the exact same four letter word, but didn't make it onto the shelves until 2006, when the song was part of a bonus CD with the girls' best-of album. But the critics loved it. Pete Paphides of *The Times* was impressed, comparing it to high-brow musical predecessors as removed from the pop realm as is humanly possible in his review of the album. 'It's as though Brian Higgins and his Xenomania songwriting team have set out to flout the rules of great pop,' he mused. 'If it didn't have *FHM* cover stars singing on it, the wah-wah nausea of 'Swinging London Town' would sit happily between Mirwais and Vitalic on your favourite synth-wonk mix CD. An album stuffed with more hooks than a mere mortal could resist.' Michael Deacon of the *Daily Telegraph* was just as complimentary: 'Girls Aloud haven't, in press-release parlance, 'matured' or 'progressed' – they've simply got much, much better.' The girls were delighted by the reception *Chemistry* had been given. Kimberley said, 'I don't know what it is, we just seem to have done really well. People thought we wouldn't get past our first album, but now here we are on our third.'

'See The Day' hit the shops a week later on 12 December, the girls' third cover version since their inception in November 2002. The video was a simple Christmas-tinged affair – snowfall, white dresses and sultry expressions. Girls Aloud were in a snow-dome, with certain words from the song highlighted in large letters behind them during the shoot. It was similar in set-up to the 'I'll Stand By You' video – a real paired-down affair. 'See The Day' charted at number nine, and broke the record formerly held by the Spice Girls for their unbroken run of ten top ten singles; Girls Aloud now had 11. The single became the girls' biggest hit on radio airplay, overtaking 2002's 'Sound Of The Underground'.

For Nicola, the salvo of releases was something of a personal triumph. Songs she had written made it onto the B sides of both the 'Biology' and 'See The Day' singles – 'Nobody But You' and 'I Don't Really Hate You' respectively. Album track 'It's Magic', while credited to Girls Aloud on the Chemistry album sleeve, is widely believed to have been written by Nicola.

By the end of the year, Girls Aloud's position as, what Cheryl once dubbed 'pop at its best', was well and truly cemented. Just before the end of the year, they managed to gain some notoriety through an over-zealous fan. A man in Walsall, West Midlands, was forced to fork out over £1,700 for playing the hits of Girls Aloud at an excessive volume after being prosecuted by local Environmental Health Officers. Clearly, *Chemistry* wasn't just a hit with the critics – the fans loved it too, even to excess.

CHAPTER 16

2006: Keeping Pop Alive

THE YEAR BEGAN with a focus on the band's diminutive Geordie. Not only was Cheryl voted the celebrity the Sun readers would like to see adorning the infamous Page Three, but she caught the eye of a top British politician – and it wasn't to be the last time Girls Aloud would marry the worlds of pop and politics in one fell swoop. Cheryl was named the winner of Celebrity Page Three Idol in January, but in a marginally more high-brow achievement, was chosen by Conservative Party leader David Cameron as his favourite member of the band. Asked which member of Girls Aloud was his favourite by Colin and Edith on Radio 1, he replied, 'The dark haired one.' Despite his distinct unfamiliarity with the nuances of the quintet, by the end of 2006, Girls Aloud had well and truly stamped their indelible imprint in the public consciousness.

But the pop scene was at breaking point. 'Pop is basically dead,' opined Cheryl, 'We're keeping it alive.'

While Girls Aloud were almost single-handling fanning the flame of an entire musical genre, pop wasn't in a great state. Iconic pop bulwark *Smash Hits* was on the verge of collapse, *Top Of The Pops* was coughing and spluttering its way through the TV schedules, but there were more surprises to come.

Before the nominations for the annual Brit awards were announced, the girls were buoyant and looking forward to competing against their pop rivals to land one of the coveted silver gongs. Franz Ferdinand frontman Alex Kapranos even sung the group's praises, surmising that Girls Aloud should romp home in the Best British Single category thanks to the might of Xenomania. He said, 'We really like Girls Aloud. There is some good song writing from whoever is writing for them. Out of all that lot of pop acts, we definitely rate the girls as the best.' But the euphoria was to be short lived. When the nominations were announced on 10 January, Girls Aloud were nowhere to be seen. James Blunt, Westlife, Katie Melua, Kelly Clarkson and Madonna made up the Best Pop Act shortlist, much to the band's disdain. 'It's become so American,' said Sarah. 'Look at the Best Pop category. It's the likes of Madonna, who isn't British. Kelly Clarkson isn't British either. It doesn't give British pop acts like us a chance.' Other musicians were up in arms with the lack of recognition for the band. Singer Richard Archer, of Hard-Fi said, 'I'm not really a pop fan but when it's done right it's good. Girls Aloud and Sugababes both do it well so it's a bit of a surprise they aren't in the pop act selection when Blunt and Melua are. They should be.'

Luckily, the band was busy preparing for their first visit Down Under, and didn't have to spend much time worrying about their pop prowess as seen through the eyes of high-powered industry folk. The darlings of the British music scene, Arctic Monkeys, were so enamoured of the band, they performed a cover version of 'Love Machine' in Radio 1's *Live Lounge* for DJ Jo Whiley, which was high praise indeed. 'It's a really good cover,' said Cheryl. 'They're genuine, they really meant it. They probably just thought it was a good song. They're great and I actually heard that when it went out on Radio 1. I thought it sounded brilliant... almost better than ours!'

Keeping Kimberley's mind off the disappointment was the honour of having a bus named after her in her hometown of Bradford. School children in Bingley had been asked to come up with a name for a new school vehicle, and in honour of the area's most famous daughter, the unanimous choice was to name it after Ms Walsh. But the fivesome's hectic schedule meant they had to cancel one of their regular January appearances – at the Cheerios Childline gig in Dublin – after it emerged the dates had been double booked; a day of filming had been pencilled in for the same date. Nadine explained, 'It's an absolute nightmare and we're really sorry we can't perform there. We had a video shoot booked in London and there was a mix-up with the dates. I was really looking forward to coming home to perform and the rest of the girls were excited too.'

Despite the disappointment, the girls soon had another part of the world to conquer – the Southern

Hemisphere. They jetted off to Sydney to launch themselves to an Aussie audience, who seemed to warm to Girls Aloud almost immediately. 'The anonymity is quite refreshing,' said Nicola. 'It's a challenge. We're willing to work hard. There's no room for laziness.' So Kimberley, Nadine, Nicola, Cheryl and Sarah embarked on a whirlwind tour of media exposure, meeting journalists, TV presenters and even the odd fan in their battle for publicity. Die-hard fans of the band, Emily Taylor and Lang Watkin had sent the group a 'big and tacky card' asking for tickets to Girls Aloud's forthcoming UK tour; not only did the pair receive the tickets in question, but were invited to meet the band on the set of Australian breakfast TV show *Sunrise* and at a visit to Sydney's Taronga Zoo. According to local press reports, a koala decided to urinate on one of the girls at the zoo, which resulted in a swift costume change before the next engagement.

Girls Aloud were well aware no visit Down Under would be complete without a trip to the set of long-running soap *Neighbours* in Melbourne – a 12 hour drive away from Sydney. They paid a visit to the fictional suburb of Erinsborough to take a walk down Ramsay Street. 'It looks really surreal,' admitted Kimberley. The band performed an impromptu rendition of the show's theme tune, and got to meet Dr Karl Kennedy, AKA Alan Fletcher – who announced he would soon be touring the UK with his band The Waiting Room – and that he was familiar with Girls Aloud. Nadine was starstruck: 'I can't believe Alan knew who we were.'

However, it wasn't the zeitgeist's potential dream collaboration that attracted the attention of the press; rather, it was the rumoured romance between *Desperate Housewives* star Jesse Metcalfe and a certain young lady from Derry. The pair met at a Sydney bar and swapped numbers, but as the actor misplaced Nadine's digits, he spent the next day tracking her down to the Four Seasons hotel. Despite admitting to a crush on the star, Nadine played it cool with the Hollywood hunk – but her father soon confirmed the pair were dating. Niall confessed, 'They have been out a few times and she likes him. She said a couple of times that she wasn't interested in men, but if the gardener from *Desperate Housewives* was free then she'd change her mind, so it is a bit spooky.'

In March, Cheryl's husband-to-be Ashley Cole was dogged by rumours he had been part of a gay orgy. The month before, the *Sun* and the *News Of The World* published claims two anonymous footballers and a DJ had indulged in homosexual acts while dropping thinly-veiled hints Ashley was involved – leading internet speculation to name Cheryl's husband-to-be as one of the unnamed players. Ashley launched legal proceedings against the newspapers over claims of harassment, breach of privacy and libel. His solicitor Graham Shearer branded the allegations 'disgraceful' in the run up to his client's wedding to Cheryl. 'These proceedings were commenced because these newspapers published false and offensive articles designed to tell readers that Ashley had behaved in what the *News Of The World* described as a 'perverted' way with other professional footballers. The newspapers knew there was no basis to name Ashley but arranged the articles and pictures in such a way that readers would identify him. There is no truth whatsoever in these allegations. Ashley Cole will not tolerate this kind of cowardly journalism or let it go unchallenged.' In June, Ashley received an apology and was awarded undisclosed damages by the publications involved. The apology read, 'We are happy to make clear that Mr Cole and [DJ] Masterstepz were not involved in any such activities. We apologise to them for any distress caused and we will be paying them each a sum by way of damages.'

Another Cheryl-related misdemeanour occurred when Mike Skinner of The Streets sparked rumours his song 'When You Wasn't Famous' – which details a previous relationship with a crack-smoking popstrel and his surprise at her prolific drug habit – was about the singer. He dedicated a performance of the song on music show *Top Of The Pops*, saying, 'This one's dedicated to Cheryl Tweedy,' but later claimed he had only done so because she happened to be in the studio at the same time, and was nothing to do with the revealing track.

Things came full circle for the girls in a reality TV sisterhood fashion when they made an appearance on Davina McCall's eponymous BBC One chat show on 8 March, sharing the bill with glamour model Jordan and jovial TV personality Eamonn Holmes. The six sassy ladies reunited almost four years since the fateful day when *Popstars: The Rivals* host Davina named Cheryl,

Nicola, Nadine, Kimberley and Sarah as the five females about to skyrocket their way to chart stardom. Each glamorously kitted out in spangly dresses and killer heels, the girls sashayed onto the set of Davina's first foray into the world of the chat show oeuvre, with the star confessing, 'I feel like your sort of musical midwife. I kind of gave birth to you in a reality TV sort of way.' And the memories of a stress-fuelled time together during the filming of *Popstars: The Rivals* came back in an instant for the girls. 'That show was a very emotional show for all of us. One thing that stuck out was how much everyone really wanted to get into that band. It meant so much to all of you,' Davina recalled. The fivesome had sweated and toiled with the *Big Brother* helmer at their side – with her becoming more like a Big Sister to the band all the way from the audition process up until the birth of the Girls Aloud in November 2002.

Ever the democratic diplomat, the girls' former mentor gave them their right to reply to an outburst earlier in the series by Welsh *Voice of An Angel* Charlotte Church, who claimed she could perform a Girls Aloud tune 'ten times better than they ever could'. While trying to tow a largely non-committal line when asked if they would gladly do karaoke to Charlotte's seminal August 2005 hit 'Crazy Chick', outspoken Cheryl was having none of her bandmates' polite deference. Sarah conceded the soprano's first opera breakaway track was 'a belter', with the others wholeheartedly agreeing with a polite, but unanimous 'yes' offered up in response. Never one to mince her words, it was Cheryl who wanted to make her true feelings heard by almost three million viewers. She retorted, 'Yeah, I'd sing it, and I'd sing it much better.' Fearing a full scale inter-pop starlet feud was brewing, Davina stepped in to diffuse the scene, pleading with the feisty Newcastle lass to keep schtum: 'No – you're more grown up than that. I trained you well.'

Davina made no secret of her love of Nadine's singing voice, even admitting she wanted her to perform 'Fields Of Gold' – one of her *Popstars* final songs – at a renewal of her wedding vows with husband Matthew Robertson in the future. Perhaps it was these thoughts of romance which spurred Davina on to set up the single bandmates with potential male suitors. Despite Nadine's now fledgling romance with Jesse, Davina played matchmaker with Nadine and Sarah, attempting to set them up with Northern Irish comic Patrick Kielty. But common homeland ties weren't enough for Ms Coyle, whose thoughts were clearly on her new romance with her very own *Desperate Housewives* hunk, who she had begun dating just the month before. While the public decided Davina's guise as a chat-show host wasn't to be a ratings success – the programme was dropped after an eight-episode run – Girls Aloud continued to go from strength to strength – despite their self-styled 'musical midwife' falling on difficult times.

The same month it was announced that all future Girls Aloud releases would be dealt with by new Polydor imprint, Fascination; Sophie Ellis-Bextor would also be making the leap to the newly christened label. On 5 March, the girls' 12th single, 'Whole Lotta History' was released. It was the fourth single to be taken from *Chemistry*, but the band's 'people' didn't have absolute confidence in the track doing as well as their previous efforts. Rachel Cooke, PR executive for Polydor, said at the time, "Whole Lotta History' doesn't feel like it's doing as well as some of the other singles have done in the past.' The video shoot took place in January on location in Paris, and was the band's first video shot outside of London. The band oozed Parisian chic and richness in the video – Kimberley having coffee in a café, Nicola gazing into a mirror, Nadine in a study, Cheryl looking resplendent on a bed, and Sarah strolling along a river Seine-side path before all having a bit of a sing-song together in someone's posh front lounge. But the girls weren't too happy with the end result. Nicola took issue with the amount of cosmetic enhancements she was sporting on her face, saying at the first playback, 'I hate the make-up. Look how much make-up I've got on – hardly anything. I hate it.' But Poppy Stanton, product manager at Polydor, admitted at least one negative reaction was to be expected. 'It's really difficult getting five girls looking gorgeous all at the same time,' she explains, 'and [make] them all happy with themselves.'

The song initially charted at number 80 the Sunday prior to its release date of 13 March, thanks to a new rule brought in for the UK charts. The new ruling allowed singles to enter the chart on download sales only, a week before the song's physical release. The week after, the song took the number six spot, continuing the band's unbroken run of top ten hits.

Despite its chart position, 'Whole Lotta History' was actually the lowest-selling Girls Aloud single in its first week, selling 11,270 copies. Cheryl penned the single's non-album B-side, 'Crazy Fool'.

The group travelled up to Gateshead to perform at a bash in aid of the Rainbow Trust, a children's charity, and sang five songs for hundreds of guests. 'We are really excited about performing for such a good cause. It's extra special because I'm performing on home ground.' Despite showing a united front on Cheryl's home turf, yet again rumours abounded of trouble in the Girls Aloud ranks – and this time it was Nadine who was allegedly on the move to launch a solo career. In February, Irish press reports had claimed the singer had been offered a secret six-figure pay deal to refrain from leaving the group, but one month later, apparently, Nadine had had enough. Manager Louis Walsh stepped in to reassure fans that it was the media who were behind the false 'will-she-won't-she' hoopla. 'Nadine isn't leaving the group,' he said. 'I've picked the songs for the next album and Nadine is in. I don't know where the rumours have started but she isn't walking out on the rest of the girls. She's happy to be in the band. I know some newspapers are making a big deal that she will have a solo deal once the band is finished, but every singer tries to continue their career beyond a band.' Nadine's dad Niall also poured cold water on the current rumour-mongering: 'I was talking to Nadine yesterday and she doesn't know where the rumour is coming from. She's happy in Girls Aloud.

The band are just back from Australia and she's having a great time at the moment.'

Meanwhile, Cheryl was feeling the strain of attempting to arrange her wedding in the summer in the midst of tour preparations and her fiancé Ashley's involvement with the football World Cup so much so she was seriously considering an elopement as the solution to all her problems. 'It's seriously stressful – it's like another full time job,' she inferred. 'I felt like I'm living with a phone glued to my ear. Right now I'm starting to think I should jack it all in and Ashley and I should run off and elope somewhere. I just want it to be him and me, alone on a beach – but I know my mum would kill me if I did it.' At the premiere of fellow Geordies Ant McPartlin and Declan Donnelly's new movie *Alien Autopsy* in London's Leicester Square, she confided, 'It's lovely to be able to take an evening off and chill out.'

In April, the girl's six part TV series *Girls Aloud: Off The Record* debuted on E4. Cameras had been following the girls every move since the New Year, and were still with the band as it travelled to China to promote London abroad. The girls were a little apprehensive about the footage which made it to the final cut, including them having a few drinks on their trip to Sydney – but the new series late-night billing at 10:30pm meant it was aimed at older fans. 'It's not a good idea to show a young audience us getting drunk and making it look like fun,' said Cheryl. 'We have to be aware of all that. If I'd seen someone I looked up to at that age being drunk and having fun, I would have probably gone out and bought a bottle of wine.' Kimberley's sister Sally said, 'It's definitely aimed at older audiences because there are clips that see them all letting their hair down and enjoying a few drinks. But it's on late at night and I don't think there is any danger of the young fans being corrupted. We are all really proud of Kimberley and know what a sensible girl she is so we aren't worried about what the documentary includes.' After the show was filmed, there were mixed feelings about the project. Kimberley said, 'The best thing about doing that show was that we've got six months of our lives logged for when we're older, and I know we're going to appreciate that.' But Cheryl was marginally more upset over the way she was portrayed, most notably during a trip up a mountainside in Athens when she got rather annoyed by a long walk. 'It [was] a little bit annoying, to be honest with you. There are times that we say, "Can you go away please?" People said I was complaining all the time,' says Cheryl, 'but a lot of it was the way they edited the footage. They make it look like you can only be bothered to climb five steps when you've actually climbed 5000.'

While Sarah, Kimberley, Nicola, Nadine and Cheryl were appearing on TV screens in the UK, they were busy in Shanghai with Mayor of London, Ken Livingstone. In a bid to strengthen economic relations between the two cities, the band travelled halfway across the world to sing a few songs for the Chinese audience as specially designated 'cultural ambassadors'.

Their performance at the 'London Fusion' event saw them do a short set in front of the invited audience, the English National Ballet danced and Chinese *Pop Idol*-style contest *Supergirl* 2005 winner Li Yuchun also sang to the crowd during the two-hour concert. It was an ideal opportunity to showcase the band to a prospective audience of 400 million. Fans gathered outside the venue on Shanghai's Bund riverside, but they weren't there to catch a glimpse of the UK's talent; the crowd of young Chinese teens were there for Yuchun. 'We don't care about London. We're coming to see Li Yuchun,' a young female student is quoted as saying. After coming off-stage following the showcase, Nadine branded the concert as 'the worst performance Girls Aloud had ever done', while Kimberley admitted she didn't think the group's brand of flirtatious pop and skimpy attire had gone down well: '[Our] sexy moves – they'll think we're all whores.' But Ken Livingstone was impressed by the girl's show, and congratulated them on a job well done. Cheryl says, 'We did catch him dancing away while we were on stage. It was one of them uncle dances, just jiggling his shoulders. He was having fun but he didn't want anyone to see him!'

Despite their bad feeling about the gig, the girls were excited about being in a different country and culture, especially Nadine. 'We came here because we just want to be involved. I love things like this,' she said. 'I love going abroad, I love seeing different places and seeing all different walks of life. This is my first time in China so it's a great opportunity for me. The food's lovely and fresh. My favourite part was visiting a Buddhist temple. It was a humbling experience. Me and Sarah got on our knees and pretended to know what to do. I like the fact that although we have a fan base out here, it's not huge and we can walk around like tourists.' But her fellow bandmates weren't as impressed. Nicola lamented the food wasn't as good as her local Chinese takeaway, and found herself confused by what culinary delights were on offer. 'The food is a bit funny,' she says. 'I asked for chow mein, and I got strawberries. Apparently chow mein means strawberries in Chinese.' Cheryl added, 'I wouldn't go on holiday there. It's a nice place to see and a nice experience, but it rained all the time. I like somewhere with more sun.'

Nadine's comments about the fabulous cuisine in China wasn't enough to stop the media speculating she had an eating disorder – something the singer was keen to dispel. She had dropped over half a stone from 8 stone, 3 pounds to 7 stone, 7 pounds since starting the band, but insisted she didn't have any problems with food. Louis Walsh had been quoted as saying, 'All the girls are small, but she is the thinnest. I worry about her. I've spoken to her as I thought she looked very skinny.' But tiny size six Nadine wasn't pleased with the comments. 'I'm happy with the way I look,' she said. 'Everyone's entitled to do whatever the hell they want to. It's not like I'm saying, 'I'm fat', so the criticism doesn't bother me. My legs are always going to be skinny. There's nothing I can do about it.'

Career-wise, it was announced in April that a

compilation of the girls' greatest hits would be released at the end of 2006 as their fourth album. Tour rehearsals were in full swing for their first ever arena tour in May, and Kimberley, Nadine, Cheryl, Nicola and Sarah were excited by the prospect of their biggest ever show. 'It's arenas that we'll be playing so we can do something on a larger scale,' explained Kimberley. 'We only start rehearsals on Monday so even we aren't sure what's happening, but we have different choreography. Last time we did 30 dates – this time it's only 10 so we can give it our all. The best part of what we do is being on the road.' Under the creative guidance of choreographer Beth Honan, the girls and their backing dancers sweated and toiled – all the while in high heels – their way through 19 different dance routines in time for next month's tour. While they were busy holed up in the dance studio, the girls took their places in *FHM*'s 100 Sexiest Women poll. Cheryl came in at number six, Sarah at 15, Nadine at 55, Kimberley at 66 and Nicola at 84.

All the girls' practice made perfect on the first night of the tour in Nottingham on 22 May. Nadine announced to the crowd, 'I just can't believe that four years on, we're doing an arena tour!' Sarah added, 'We're so excited we can't breathe!' Sophie Heawood, writing in the *Guardian*, was particularly impressed by Cheryl's shouty-singing hybrid during a cover of Kaiser Chiefs 'I Predict A Riot': 'Footballer's fiancée she might be, but there's no Posh Spice-style miming in the background for Cheryl Tweedy. During 'I Predict a Riot', it seems brave enough to give the famous nightclub brawler the lines about people getting lairy. When she decides to stop singing and start shouting, it's hilarious and utterly brilliant.' The *Daily Telegraph* was equally as complimentary about the girls' pop makeover of the indie tune, although was slightly perplexed by the change in lyrics from 'borrow a pound for a condom' to 'borrow a pound for a phonecall' as it was too risqué for the group's young fans. 'It was an excellent, rapturous version,' wrote reviewer Michael Deacon, 'Although it is curious that, to protect the innocence of younger fans, they omitted the last word of the line 'Borrow a pound for a condom' – but then later sang 'She's got a PhD with her legs apart' from their own 'Racy Lacey'.' Cheryl's rap during 'Watch Me Go' was something to behold – the diminutive singer looked and sounded like she was having the time of her life.

The *Chemistry* Tour setlist consisted of:
'Biology'
'No Good Advice'
'Waiting'
'Love Machine'
'Long Hot Summer'
'Whole Lotta History'
'Watch Me Go'
'I Predict a Riot'
'See The Day'
'Sound Of The Underground'
Medley from the musicals: '*Fame*', '*What A Feeling*' and '*Footloose*'

'The Show'
'Intro'
'Models'
'Racy Lacey'
'I'll Stand By You'
'Biology' (reprise)
'Wild Horses'
'Wake Me Up'
'Jump'

Cheryl got an overwhelming reception when Girls Aloud played on Tyneside. According to reports, every time the Geordie's face appeared on-screen, fans would scream and chant 'Cheryl, Cheryl' in support of the star. She told the crowd, 'I'm so overwhelmed I can't even talk. I told the girls you would be the best crowd and I wasn't wrong. I'm so proud to be a Geordie tonight. You really are the best. This is a dream come true to perform here in front of my friends and family.' Cheryl later admitted the tour had been the highlight of her year. 'The *Chemistry* tour was amazing,' she said, 'Our first arena tour and it was a sell-out. To us, it was like having a party every night.'

Nadine's family squeezed in a surprise 21st birthday for the Derry girl in Newcastle, carting over countless friends and family from Northern Ireland in the Girls Aloud tour bus for the big day as due to work commitments, celebrating on 15 June wasn't a feasible option. 'We realised Newcastle was the only gig where she would have a day off the next day so we arranged the surprise party for her at the Malmaison Hotel and brought 40 family and friends over from Derry to join the stars,' explained dad Niall. 'It was even to the point where she was upset and thought no-one cared, and was saying things like the family didn't even come over for the tour. She just couldn't believe it [when they turned up], we were all there with the band, crew and dancers.' Jesse Metcalfe and Nadine's relationship was going from strength to strength, with Nadine confessing. 'Things are going great with Jesse – he's a fantastic guy. We're taking things slowly, but we are enjoying each other's company. And he's pretty, which always helps.' The fact he splashed out on a £30,000 bracelet from Tiffany for her 21st probably helped too.

In June after the tour drew to a close, it was a case of another month, and another member of the band allegedly packing their bags and leaving the Girls Aloud show. Sarah was rumoured to have 'had enough' of the group and had expressed her desire to quit. Again, the band were forced to step forward and end the speculation. 'No-one's ever threatened to quit,' said Nadine. 'If they did, the rest of us would be like, "okay, go on." Then seconds later they'd come back and say they didn't want to.' She added the band had a way of dealing with feuds: 'It's a democracy. If three of us agree on something, we'll go with what they want.'

The *Sun* newspaper printed a picture of Kimberley allegedly smoking a joint, taken in December 2005 at a friend's party. Kimberley apologised to her fans, but her father John later told local paper the *Telegraph and Argus* that the story had been exaggerated. He said, 'This has been twisted. This was not a joint, it was a rolled-up cigarette. It was not even lit and there is no smoke coming out. She was passing it across the room and put it in her mouth as a bit of a laugh. It's important that she should not be portrayed that way – it's not the truth.' He also claimed his daughter had been forced into making an apology regardless of whether she was smoking cannabis or not. 'The paper said it would be running the story and that it would be best if she just apologised otherwise they would make it sound worse.' She told the *Sun* she was mortified because her fans may think she was smoking drugs. But the *Sun* showbiz reporter Victoria Newton claimed Kimberley's dad's accusations were false. She said, 'Kimberley confirmed that it was a spliff and that is why she apologised.' Kimberley later said of the incident, 'It hardly makes me Pete Doherty.'

The same month, it was announced Cheryl would wed fiancé Ashley Cole six days after the World Cup final, on 15 July. Cheryl flew into Baden Baden in Germany on 9 June prior to England's first game against Paraguay – on a budget airline, hardly befitting her celebrity status. 'I didn't realise we were flying with Ryanair. I think it's quite funny. I just hope he's booked us into a nice hotel,' she quipped. 'I've got to pop back for a few gigs and things but I'll be there for all the games. I think they'll win it. I'm very confident. He's very confident.' While the Wives And Girlfriends wagon had well and truly rolled into town at the five-star Brenner Park Hotel, Cheryl intimated she wouldn't be heading out on the razz with her fellow football widows. 'I prefer to pamper myself just sitting in the bath.'

It was during the World Cup Cheryl reignited her friendship with Victoria Beckham, with the pair preferring to distance themselves from the other WAGs. 'I love Victoria,' she said. 'She's just so witty and down to earth. She's from a girl band and she's not a typical footballer's wife. She's very ambitious so we have a lot in common.' The pair dined together on several occasions and spent hours chatting in each others' hotel rooms, comparing notes on their respective girl band experiences. 'The Spice Girls had to work twice as hard as we do because they did America and the whole shebang in no time,' says Cheryl. 'When I was sitting next to Victoria at the World Cup, she was like, "Are you sure it's all right for you to be here? Shouldn't you be doing a gig or something?" Another time she said, "We were just like you lot, Cheryl: five random girls auditioned and thrown together."' They effectively distanced themselves from the all-conquering raucous gaggle of the other WAGs. Naturally, the papers began speculating a move to Madrid, with Ashley transferring to Spanish football giants – and David Beckham's then team – Real Madrid, was on the cards.

Cheryl took the opportunity to make her feelings about the others heard, but later claimed her comments had been taken out of context. 'Footballers' wives have no careers and live off their husbands' money. You see girls in clubs making a beeline for the footballers and it makes me sick. Everyone's so flash. It's like, "Who's got the best watch on, who's got the best bag, which wife is dressed the best, which has got the best hair?" I'm like, "I've got my own career". I'll sit back and read the mags. I've got my own money, so if my husband's card gets declined, I just whip out mine. Footballers' wives are just as bad as benefit scroungers – it's just a higher class of sponger.' The first of July saw England knocked out of the World Cup, so the team returned home with their WAGs in tow to drown their sorrows. However, Cheryl was whisked straight from Baden Baden to a photoshoot for the press campaign for new 'bloke Coke' Coke Zero, of which she was the new face.

It soon emerged that the British music scene's great young hope Lily Allen had immortalised Cheryl in one of her songs. While it later transpired Lily was being tongue-in-cheek when she sang 'I wish I looked like Cheryl Tweedy', the track – presumably not heard by Cheryl or else she would have realised it had more than a whiff of satire – moved the Girls Aloud star to praise the pop star's own good looks. 'I'm really flattered that Lily's written a track about me,' said Cheryl. 'But I don't know why she sings about wanting to be as pretty as me, as she looks stunning. I'd like to look like that.'

Just before the wedding, soon-to-be husband and wife team Cheryl and Ashley got together to promote a new National Lottery game. Dismissed as a 'tacky stunt' by many, the shoot to promote the Dream Number draw saw the couple clad in white posing beside a Rolls Royce to lure lotto players to the apparently ethereal game. Cheryl drew upon her own experiences of luck to sell the draw to any disbelievers. 'All in all, I've been really lucky in my career with people saying "yes" to give me a chance,' she said, 'So here's hoping that someone else's lucky number comes up this weekend too.' In the run up to the wedding, Ashley and his pals headed to Puerto Banus in Spain for their stag weekend, while Cheryl enjoyed nights on the tiles closer to home – namely in London club Umbaba, where she partied the night away with her bandmates and her best friend, her mum Joan.

The wedding itself, on 15 July, was a splendid affair – and there were rumours Cheryl's beloved Chihuahua Buster would accompany her up the aisle in a specially commissioned wedding outfit. With a £1 million deal with *OK!* Magazine in the bag, the Coles did their best to throw rival paparazzi off the scent, pretending their celebration would take place in Highclere Castle, the same venue chosen by Jordan and Peter Andre for their 2005 nuptials. In actual fact, the wedding took place at posh stately home Wrotham Park, where the couple's friends and family – and of course the rest of Girls Aloud – witnessed the showbiz wedding of the year before Mr and Mrs Cole headed off into the sunset for their honeymoon in the Seychelles. The wedding bells spurred on the press to speculate Nicola, Kimberley and Nadine were gearing up to tie the knot with their respective partners, but each girl was quick to dispel the rumours. Most high-profile was the prospect of Nadine and Jesse's wedding, but Nadine was quick to deny the rumours. 'The wedding was just brilliant,' she said. 'We couldn't really believe it was happening. We were all at the back getting our dresses on and in a way it felt like we were getting ready to shoot a video. Then suddenly Cheryl was walking down to get married. It was wonderful and she looked stunning. Jesse's just lovely. But we don't have any plans to settle down just yet. No way. We're just enjoying ourselves.'

Jesse soon met the Coyle clan, and the family was suitably impressed. Dad Niall admitted he was taken aback by 'how down-to-earth' Jesse was after their first meeting. 'We were all out the night before and he had plenty to drink and was a bit tipsy, having a good time,' he explains. 'The next morning he got up and we were all having a good craic. We had a big fry-up and after Jesse collected everyone's plates and did all the washing up. To me that said a lot about the kind of guy he is and how he was brought up.'

With the Coyle-pleasing boyfriend in the bag, Nadine was also feeling rather triumphant – not only had she just been named Ireland's Sexiest Woman in a poll conducted by saucy sexual unguent retailer Ann Summers, but a series of charity gigs in aid of the Northern Ireland Children's Hospice – of which Nadine was an ambassador – had been arranged in Derry for the first time, at the city's Millennium Forum in August. She couldn't wait to perform for a home crowd. She said, 'I'm so excited, the opportunity has never been here before. I've been to the hometowns of all the other girls so now it's my turn. The girls have a vision of Ireland and they imagine we all live in thatched cottages. I think they're going to be in for a shock. I love getting home but don't get to do it that often. My family usually come to London to see me. That's why this gig at the Forum means so much to me.' The August concerts came days after an acclaimed performance at the V Festival – normally the sole preserve of indie kids, established rockers and hip artists... not the usual haunt of a pop act. But the girls threw themselves in to their performance, with many fans being turned away from the festival's JJB Sports/Puma tent where the band was playing because they had been an unprecedented success – and it was Cheryl's first official gig as Mrs Cole. She admits, 'We were shitting ourselves thinking people were going to hate us but the tent we played at was packed and they had to shut it because it was over-crowded. We were playing the same day as Radiohead and Keane. We couldn't believe it.'

Girls Aloud's busy calendar over the summer saw them co-host an episode of Channel Four's *The Friday Night Project* with Alan Carr and Justin Lee Collins, launch a range of shampoos with haircare company Sunsilk, and take some well-earned rest overseas after the usual slew of outdoor gigs. Just before the first August concert in Derry, Nadine's dad Niall spoke of his daughter's feelings about playing in Derry for the first time in the band's four-year history. 'I was talking to her about half an hour ago and she is busting with excitement. She is really nervous too because this is her home crowd. The other girls are really excited and can't wait to get here because they have heard a lot about Derry.' The concert was a resounding success, with Girls

Aloud doing a brief question and answer session with the audience midway through the set – during which Nadine's bandmates admitted when they first met Nadine, they had terrible trouble deciphering her Derry accent. After the gig, Nadine visited kids at the Northern Ireland Children's Hospice, to whom a percentage of the proceeds from the local concerts were going. Her ambassadorial role came about after witnessing the work of the charity first hand, with six-year-old Caitlin Deacon, a child of a family friend attending the hospice. 'Kerry [Caitlin's mother] asked me to consider it and I haven't ever been an ambassador for any charity before. I just thought, "If you let me, I would love to be involved."' Patricia O'Callaghan, of the Hospice, said, 'We are thrilled that Nadine was able to visit us today and we are so proud that she is our ambassador. We know when she leaves here she will fly the flag of the hospice wherever she goes.'

However, Girls Aloud's Northern Irish odyssey was to end on a sour note for fans. A special show at The Elk nightclub in Toomebridge, County Antrim, was slated to take place on 3 September, but was cancelled 'in the interest of customers' after it emerged the local press, cameras and even mobile phones would be banned. The band's manager Hilary Shaw was disappointed by the unfortunate end to Girls Aloud's extended visit to Northern Ireland. She said, 'To be honest, I don't know why this was cancelled. The press people don't want us to do interviews or pictures before the launch of the greatest hits album but after that it is fine. There is a whole strategy in place and we have to abide by that. They cancelled. We didn't.'

On the band's return to London, it was announced that Sarah was to become the new face of Scots-based lingerie brand Ultimo in a £100,000 deal, joining the ranks of supermodel Helena Christensen, Rachel Hunter and Penny Lancaster. Earlier in the year, manager Hilary Shaw had quipped, 'We could get a lot of endorsements – especially for thongs – now,' after snaps of Sarah in a bikini were published in a newspaper; and Hilary's word had foretold the future. 'When ([Ultimo creator] Michelle [Mone] asked me to become the new face and body of the brand, I was so honoured and extremely excited,' said Sarah. 'I loved working with her and the team. The Ultimo lingerie is gorgeous.' Ms Mone herself reciprocated the singer's thoughts: 'Sarah had never modelled before, however she was fantastic on the day of the shoot. She was signed to appeal to a younger market and to further demonstrate Ultimo's ability to enhance a woman's confidence, both inside and out.' Another solo project for Sarah was a small role in a new movie. Throughout her career with Girls Aloud, Sarah made it known she was keen on acting, and being offered a part in gangster movie *Bad Day* alongside Donna Air and Claire Goose was a dream come true. 'I just wanted to do something different. All the other girls have done magazine shoots and I wanted to do my own thing. I only had to take three days out of our schedule to learn my lines and then a day to film it. It's only a short role and I'm really nervous it will end up on the cutting-room floor. I insisted on wearing a brown wig for the role because I didn't want to look like Sarah from Girls Aloud. I had to sit in the back of a cab, swearing down the phone – it's not like me at all!'

October also saw the release of the girls first new single from their forthcoming greatest hits album, *The Sound Of Girls Aloud*. 'Something Kinda Ooh' was a high-octane crazy-worded romp taking its cues from 1990s rave beats. The video saw the girls posing in and pretending to drive high performance convertible cars, against a moving backdrop of London by night. The driving scenes were intercut with footage of the girls' silhouettes against bright neon lights and footage of the girls dancing en masse – with possibly the best dance move ever, which involved lifting their right leg and patting their bottom to the words *'Something kinda ooh/Jumping on my tutu'*. Kimberley unveiled a new curly hairstyle, debuted during the girls' *Chemistry* tour a few months back. Following its release on 23 October, the single reached number three in the charts – Girls Aloud's highest chart position since 'I'll Stand By You' in December 2004. A week later, the girls' greatest hits package, *The Sound Of Girls Aloud* hit the shops, giving them their first number one album, going triple platinum with over 815,000 copies sold. A special edition double CD was also released, boasting a pink front cover and eight 'rarities', including 'Singapore' – a track recorded for *Chemistry*, but which never made it on to the album; 'No Good Advice' popped up with the addition of some appropriately-placed swearing; the original version of 'Wake Me Up' with different lyrics; an extended 'TV appearance' version of 'Sound Of The Underground'; 'I Predict A Riot' as heard on tour; a rockingly riotous version of Blondie's 'Hanging On The Telephone'; ballad 'Loving Is Easy'; and the pièce de la résistance – a version of 'Sacred Trust', most recently performed by their male counterparts on *Popstars: The Rivals*, One True Voice. The critics praised the compilation, with the *Guardian* branding it 'near-faultless high-octane pop all the way', while the *Sunday Times* said, 'In league with Brian Higgins' Xenomania team, these endearingly stroppy, gobby, messy girls breeze and brawl through unimpeachable, sugar-rush pop singles. Sensational.'

Another TV show was in the pipeline for Girls Aloud, but with a difference. They were invited to do a one-off special for ITV with *Most Haunted* presenter and ex *Blue Peter* stalwart Yvette Fielding. The girls spent a night in disused Crossley Hospital morgue in Cheshire and seventeenth-century mansion, Plas Teg in Pontblyddyn, Wales. The band had a frightening time. Nadine refused to take part, saying, 'I don't want to be mixing with that kind of thing,' while Cheryl was reduced to tears by the spooky situation: 'It was terrible. I yelled the place down and burst into tears when something touched my arm.'

In November, Nadine headed to LA for crisis talks with Jesse. Despite the pair's loved-up state, the pressure of conducting a long-distance relationship had begun to take its toll. Soon after, Nicola split up with childhood sweetheart Carl Egerton. A charity collaboration with girl-band 'rivals' Sugababes was announced – Girls Aloud's most sought after singing cohorts, despite reports the two were bitter rivals. Kimberley said, 'There's no point in trying to stir up rivalries between us and the Sugababes. It's nice to have at least one other group working in the same area. There's enough room for both of us, and I respect the Sugababes for sticking around so long.' Speaking earlier in the year, Nicola said, 'If it was going to be anyone [to duet with] I guess the Sugababes would work well with us. I think we have a similar sound.' Months later, Sugababe Keisha Buchanan hinted the trio would like to team up with the fabulous fivesome. 'It would be great to get together with Girls Aloud. If we could find a song like [The Pussycat Dolls'] 'Don't Cha' or 'Lady Marmalade', then I think it could be fun.'

Meanwhile, Girls Aloud's bid for the Christmas number one came in the shape of a cover of Tommy James' 'I Think We're Alone Now', more recently covered by Eighties pop starlet Tiffany. Xenomania gave the tune a complete overhaul, added a pumping dance beat, and let the girls loose on the sing-a-long melody. The song was used on the soundtrack for new movie *It's A Boy Girl Thing,* which Cheryl and Nicola attended the premiere of in December. The video for 'I Think We're Alone Now' was based in a Los Angeles casino, with the girls attempting a five-piece heist while still managing to uphold the basic principles of glamour in their swanky outfits – including Cheryl dressed up as a magician. Customers of mobile phone network 3 were given the opportunity to download the video and three separate endings – entitled 'shocking', 'funny' and 'sexy'.

With *The X Factor* winner Leona Lewis releasing her single 'A Moment Like This' in time to be in contention for the coveted Christmas number one, it was a given that she would trounce the competition and land the top stop – which she did. Kimberley admitted, 'It's all about who will be number two now as Leona's so far ahead.' Releasing their fourth cover was a controversial move, but the girls insisted they loved the track. 'We decided to sing 'I Think We're Alone Now' because it's such a great tune and everyone can sing along to it too,' explained Nadine, 'It was our decision. There was another track suggested to us [rumoured to be Frankie Goes To Hollywood's 'The Power Of Love'], which shall forever remain a secret, but we wanted to do this. It's such a fun party song and we just wanted to do a track that was kitsch and fun.' Sarah added, 'We've given it a Girls Aloud twist, made it a bit clubbier and also brought it up to date. We didn't want to do a straightforward cover as that wouldn't be as interesting. We got a message from Tiffany saying she liked our version which we were really chuffed about.' After the song's release on 18 December, it reached number four in the charts, the girls 14th consecutive top ten single – more than any other girl group in UK chart history.

In an unprecedented move, Girls Aloud did an interview with high-brow political magazine *New Statesman* at the close of the year. The girls found it an excellent break from the usual line of questioning from journalists, and spoke passionately about their political views. 'We need to make politics more user-friendly', said an impassioned Sarah. 'It just isn't talked about in normal magazines and newspapers. We never get asked who we would vote for. It could be a general question to ask us in an interview, but it isn't.' Cheryl reckoned Westminster should let Girls Aloud get in on the political act: 'They need people like us to go into the schools and help spread the word. Our fans would definitely listen to us. They'd think, well, if Kimberley and Cheryl and Nicola are interested in it, then I want to know about it.' Cheryl also noted David Cameron 'was just trying to be cool' when he mentioned he fancied her at the beginning of the year. 'I bet he couldn't name a single song of ours,' she joked. 'Do I fancy him? No! Politicians should stop trying to be cool and get on with running the country.'

With the Christmas and New Year break upon them, Kimberley, Cheryl, Nadine, Sarah and Nicola were looking forward to the year ahead. Nadine was loved up with Jesse – who spent the festive period in Derry with the Coyles – while the rest of the girls were back up north with their families. Tickets to their greatest hits tour had sold out within days, their fifth album was in the pipeline, so Girls Aloud planned to enjoy their well-earned rest.

CHAPTER 17

Cheryl and Ashley Tie the Knot

GIRLS ALOUD'S MOST high profile love affair was that of Cheryl and her boyfriend, England footballer Ashley Cole, and it was fitting that their most high-profile outing since the *Popstars: The Rivals* days was the pair's 15 July 2006 wedding. Despite vowing never to get married after her parents Joan and Garry split up, after a 21-month courtship, the couple tied the knot in front of countless friends, family, and a select number of journalists from OK! magazine, by whom they had been paid £1 million for exclusive rights to the wedding at stately home Wrotham Park in Barnet, Hertfordshire – the backdrop for Robert Altman's movie Gosford Park (2001). The couple's big day helped make the magazine the UK's top selling gossip publication, and the two issues which covered the pair's wedding sold just over two million copies – sales figures almost unheard of for British publications.

Cheryl admitted she was nervous about going it alone without the rest of Girls Aloud, despite being flanked by her bandmates on the big day. 'I feel really strange,' she said. 'I can't get my head around it. All the girls keep ringing and screaming down the phone – it kind of feels like a big event rather than my wedding day because I'm so used to doing things as a group and it feels strange.'

Cheryl had dreamt of meeting her Prince Charming ever since she was young, and after a few dates with Ashley, she knew he was The One. She also had clear ideas what shape she wanted her nuptials to take – and there wasn't a pre-nuptial agreement in sight. She said, 'I think it's disgusting. I could understand if you're 93 and you've got billions of pounds and this 24-year-old wants to marry you in a month. But we're a work in progress, we're going to build our married life together not thinking about what if it ever ends.' Cheryl decided she wanted an angelic theme for her special day, which even included a pair of angel wings fixed to the back of her chair during the meal: 'I wanted it to be angelic because it means everything is peaceful and beautiful, and airy and light, ' she said. 'Plus Ashley always calls me his angel.' With her spectacular WAGs contacts, she enlisted the help of florist Simon Lycett, who was responsible for the floral delights at fellow girl band stalwart and WAG Victoria Beckham's wedding to David over seven years earlier in July 1999. Despite Cheryl and Ashley's wealth, Cheryl was keen not to alienate her non-celebrity friends. Lycett said, 'Cheryl didn't want her friends and family to feel intimidated and to walk in and think, "Oh

God, a great big footballer's wedding." It's very ethereal and it has a nice gentle feel to it but there will still be some wow factors.'

Cheryl held her hen night in London on the Thursday before the wedding, and the night passed without an L-plate or a novelty-shaped straw in sight. Sarah, Nadine, Nicola, Kimberley, the bride-to-be and their mums partied in the VIP section of swanky West End club Umbaba, drinking nearly £800 worth of pink champagne and cocktails until the early hours of the morning. Cheryl's mum Joan said, 'We had a great time at the hen night, it was a wild night. We all had a few drinks but Cheryl was trying to be careful on the night.'

Coming just weeks after the football World Cup in Germany, planning the wedding was something of a nightmare. Ashley was in training and playing games for England prior to the July date, while Cheryl was touring with the other girls around the UK. It was clear the couple needed someone to orchestrate their nuptials – so they chose wedding planner Katie Mash to organise proceedings – with a little help from their mobile phones. Mash says, 'It's been an absolute pleasure to work with them – and that is despite their unbelievably busy schedules leading up to the wedding, what with Cheryl on tour and Ashley in the World Cup. We've all worked around the clock and I'm definitely a pro at planning a wedding by text message now!' Cheryl admits it was a very stressful time which saw her breaking down in tears for over a month beforehand – and her future husband wasn't much help. She said, 'I had the

[*Chemistry*] tour coming up, I was working so hard, the World Cup was coming up and then on top of that I had the wedding stuff. I felt like it was on top of my shoulders, because even if there was someone else, they can't make my decisions for me because it's my wedding. I tried [to consult Ashley on] a few things in the beginning but I soon realised there was not point because he would just say, "Whatever you want, babe."'

The guest list was a celebrity booker's dream – the UK's finest pop stars and footballers were out in full force for the wedding of the year; Sugababes Keisha Buchanan, Amelle Berrabah and Heidi Range and her boyfriend, MTV presenter Dave Berry, Simon Webbe, Jamelia, and Sol Campbell. Cheryl's new pals the Beckhams weren't able to attend, but sent David's mum and sister, Sandra and Joanne, in their places. According to press reports, the invitations to non-celebrity guests included a contract banning them from pestering the celebrity contingent for autographs. The invitations also failed to mention where the wedding would be held – but a number to call two days before the nuptials was enclosed, in a bid to stop the paparazzi from ruining their big day. The couple had kept the press guessing as to where the wedding would be held, with the general tabloid consensus that the pair would tie the knot at Highclere Castle in Newbury, Berkshire, the scene of Jordan and Peter Andre's nuptials the previous year. Ashley later joked, 'We thought no-one would turn up as they were off to Highclere Castle!' And their red herring technique was a success – while the bride, groom and their 500 guests travelled to Wrotham Park, the British media were busy waiting in Berkshire for the couple.

Italian designer Roberto Cavalli was the fashionista of the day, kitting out both Ashley and Cheryl on their big day. Again, the Beckham connection was there – Cheryl's dress was the exact same frock Victoria had worn to Sir Elton John's White Tie and Tiara Ball the previous year, which was teamed with Roberto Cavalli snakeskin shoes and a diamond tiara. But the singer was keen to point out she had tracked down Cavalli of her own accord and struck up a friendship with the Italian – and not relied on the recommendation of the former Spice Girl. 'There's been loads of speculation that it was Victoria who put me in touch with Roberto Cavalli,' explained Cheryl, 'but it was actually nothing to do with her. We just both love that designer. Because we're a similar size, his clothes fit both of us like a glove. I just looked through some designs Roberto had sketched and it turned out my favourite was his favourite as well. My cousin tried on her dress and my aunt burst into tears. My dress designer doesn't speak much English and said, "Ah, she's raining!" I loved him from then on.'

As is to be expected with a high-earning footballer, Ashley was dressed to the nines in a beige tux and tails, cream suit and fancy tan shoes. Best man was Ashley's brother Matthew Cole, with ushers Cecil Talian, Jon Fortune, Paulo Vernazza and Jermaine Wynter, who first introduced Ashley to his bride.

The wedding took place at 5pm, with Ashley pulling up the church, which was festooned in lilies and hydrangeas, in a swish silver and black Rolls-Royce. Cheryl was 20 minutes late, arriving at the Holy Trinity Chapel in Bentley Heath in a luxury horse-drawn carriage – and was a bundle of nerves: 'I was panicking earlier, feeling like I couldn't breathe, partly because of the dress and partly because I was so nervous.' According to press reports, Cheryl arrived hidden under a sheet, away from prying eyes. Cheryl's brother Garry led the procession, flanked by her nephews John, Warren and Joel and Ashley's nephew Kenzie as the couple's troupe of pageboys. At such a landmark occasion in her life, Cheryl chose to share it with her bandmates, all of whom acted as bridesmaids on the day: 'I chose the girls in the band because they've been such a big part of my life now for four years, and in years to come when I look at my wedding pictures I would hate for them to be in the background as guests – they're more important than that. I want them here by my side – they've become my best friends.' As bridesmaids, the girls joined Cheryl's niece Melissa, her cousin Kelly Tweedy, and sister Gillian as maid of honour. The gaggle of girls were decked out in fancy coral frocks with a cheeky leopard print trim and leopard print sandals. Sarah, Nicola, Nadine and Kimberley were so happy to see their friend tie the knot, and were delighted Cheryl asked them to play such a big role at the wedding. Cheryl says, 'I asked them separately. Nicola cried, Kimberley screamed then cried, and Sarah and Nadine were just in shock. They thought I was going to say I was pregnant. Then when I'd asked all of them, we all had a bottle of champagne in the back of the car – the only thing we could find to drink out of were there horrible plastic cups, but it really didn't matter.' Prior to the wedding, the papers reported Girls Aloud had made a special souvenir video for Cheryl to celebrate her wedding. 'The papers said we made a compilation video tape for Cheryl as a gift but we never did,' said Nadine. 'If we'd seen that two weeks before we would have ripped off their idea!'

Nicola, one of Cheryl's best pals, admits she was in floods of tears when she first caught sight of the Geordie girl. She says, 'I cried when I saw her, then I was happy throughout the service and then I started crying at the end. When I was watching her get married I was remembering back to when we shared a room during *Popstars: The Rivals*, thinking 'she's my little girl'.' Sarah added, 'It was so lovely to see them get married because they're so in love. But it does make me think, "Argh, I'm not married yet!"' Nadine said, 'It was like she was turning into a woman right in front of me. I cried when I saw her come down the aisle, it was like she was a proper grown-up. I feel like we're all just playing at being grown ups.' Kimberley said, 'Cheryl was so excited before we left the house. She was nervous too but she was just loving the day. She and Ashley are so perfect for each other.' While Nicola and Kimberley brought their respective boyfriends, Carl Egerton and Justin Scott, as their plus ones, single girls Nadine and Sarah brought their families with them to enjoy their bandmate's special day.

The couple hired the services of a gospel choir for the evening, who sang Alicia Keys' 'If I Ain't Got You' as the bridal party sashayed up the aisle. Cheryl and Ashley had eschewed hymns in favour of contemporary, lovey-dovey songs to see out their special day, with romantic tune 'Amazed' by Lone Star sung in the middle of the service, along with soul classic 'Ain't No Mountain High Enough'.

Garry Tweedy senior walked his daughter up the aisle, and when Ashley caught sight of his bride to be, he was visibly moved – so much so her couldn't bring himself to look at Cheryl at first in case he burst into floods of tears. He said, 'I had a tear in my eye when I first saw her and then I did cry – I'm not afraid to admit it. She just looked so amazing, like a little princess.' After the vows, the pair kissed three times after being awarded their married status by the reverend, with the couple walking out of the church to the strains of 'Oh Happy Day' before hot footing it into the horse drawn carriage en route to the reception at Wrotham Park. Cheryl Tweedy had now blossomed into Mrs Cheryl Cole.

In true star style, the couple have employed the services of Rhubarb Food Design, who had catered for everyone who is anyone throwing parties in the showbiz world, and provided the food for Sir Elton John and David Furnish's civil partnership ceremony in December 2005. Like any good event, cocktails and canapés were the order of the day before the sit-down dinner later that evening, which featured steak and chips – as the couple didn't want any fancy food. Rhubarb's Lucy Gemmell says, 'They wanted something simple and delicious and exquisitely prepared. Nothing super-flash.' Thoughtful Cheryl pulled out all the stops to organise a special surprise for her beau. She arranged for superstar crooner John Legend to be flown over from the US to lend his singing skills to the first dance at the wedding disco. The pair had thoroughly enjoyed a first date spent at a gig by the singer, and Cheryl thought it would be fitting to get the man himself over to bring the memories of where it all began flooding back. But it was difficult keeping the exciting news from her husband-to-be. She admits, 'I was bursting to say something to Ashley all day but I just couldn't because I love surprises.' Ashley was astounded when Legend emerged during the opening bars of hit 'Stay With You': 'I knew there was going to be a surprise, but I had no idea what it was. I was just amazed. I'm not usually starstruck but we were both really starstruck, and we got to meet him afterwards and he was really nice. Legend said, 'Cheryl just got in touch with my management. I'd heard of Girls Aloud but not Ashley, as we don't have much soccer in the US. It's kind of funny performing at a wedding like this because you're not sure what to play, but it was a really great experience.'

The proud parents and families of both Cheryl and Ashley lined up to praise the couple. Cheryl's mum Joan was delighted by her daughter's dream wedding come true – and her choice of suitor. 'The dress looked absolutely amazing,' she said. 'but then what do you expect? She's stunning, isn't she? She could wear anything and would make it look stunning. Ashley looked very handsome in his suit too. I was very proud. He's such a kind, gentle man, and Cheryl loves him so much and he does her too. I couldn't ask for a better son-in-law.' Ashley's mum Sue was delighted by the love match, gushing, 'I'm so happy because Cheryl is such a lovely girl and they are so good together. Just look at the two of them. They're gorgeous!'

Cheryl's dad Garry was full of praise for his daughter, saying, 'When Cheryl was born, I thought I was handed an angel. It was the proudest day of my life. She's independent, smart and stunning – perfect in every way. I couldn't ask for a better daughter. What I wanted for her was a smart, sensible, reliable partner and I'm delighted Ashley is all of those things, and I'm delighted to welcome Ashley to our family.' In the spirit of the day, Garry presented Ashley with a Newcastle United football top emblazoned with 'Cole' on the back – as he dreamed his son-in-law would play for his team in the future.

Best man and Ashley's brother also lavished praise on the couple, but also gave mum Sue a special mention. 'Cheryl looked absolutely beautiful today and Ashley looked as smart as a button,' he said, 'But I'd also like to thank our mum, who has brought us up properly.'

The wedding party continued late into the evening, with disco-dancing moves aplenty. The couple had provided shisha pipes in the 'nightclub' stuffed full of flavoured tobacco for their guests to enjoy. Breakfast-style food was served at around 1am for peckish partygoers, and an hour later, Cheryl and Ashley changed out of their wedding attire to head back to their hotel for their first night as husband and wife, and then on to a luxury break in the Seychelles for their honeymoon.

Ashley told *OK!* Magazine, 'It's everything I could have wished for. Cheryl looked beautiful. I got a little emotional. When I was younger I never ever thought my wedding would be as good as this or that I'd be getting married in a house as nice as this. It's a dream come true.'

CHAPTER 18

2007: The Greatest Hits

FOR KIMBERLEY, NADINE, Nicola, Sarah and Cheryl, it looked like it was going to be a good year. Riding on the back of the success of The Sound Of Girls Aloud, the girls entered 2007 with a spring in their step after a short break over the Christmas holidays, and the news they were now the Most Successful Reality TV Group, according to fact oracle the Guinness Book Of Records. Tickets for their greatest hits tour were sold out for most of the 11 venues, with tickets changing hands on auction website eBay for hundreds of pounds – the band was well and truly in demand.

In January, a new series of *Celebrity Big Brother* had begun. Sarah had been approached to appear on the show, but turned it down: 'I'm glad I didn't go,' she later said. Her former close pal, model Danielle Lloyd, with whom she holidayed with in Dubai in 2005, appeared on the reality TV programme, but ended up garnering hundreds of negative column inches after the treatment of Bollywood star Shilpa Shetty by Jade Goody, former S Club 7 singer Jo O'Meara and Danielle became a national 'racist' issue. Sarah said, 'To be honest, I haven't spoken to [Danielle] for ages. And I haven't read anything about *Celebrity Big Brother* and what she's supposed to have said. But basically, I don't think this is a great situation for any of those girls to be in.'

Nadine made an appearance in court in the middle of the month over a drugs gang, who planned to use her north London home as a base for selling cocaine. Back in August, she had come face-to-face with four drug-dealers who hoped to run a business selling narcotics from Nadine's flat, as they thought the apartment was empty – unbeknownst to the men, Nadine had negotiated a two-week extension on her lease. She told Harrow Crown Court, 'I was sitting in the living room with my mammy. She told me there was someone coming in next door. I said, 'No way', that was my house. I went to the door and there were four men in the hall entrance. I was shocked. I was really shocked. I thought "Ooh". I was like "What are yous doing?" and the men walked out straight away and stood at the door. They said, "We are here to view your flat." The four men had thought Nadine had already moved out and the flat was empty. The next day, Nadine complained about the incident to manager Hilary Shaw, and the locks to the flat were changed. Speaking in public, Nadine was very aware of her strong Derry accent, telling the court, 'If there are any problems with my accent, just stop me.'

The men were later charged with conspiring to supply 42 kilogrammes of cocaine. The gang was later sentenced to a collective 57 years between them.

With the new year just passed, the girls' thoughts had turned to settling down. After spending the festive season with her beau Jesse Metcalfe, Nadine realised just how much she missed home. 'I would love to return home for good and set up a big house in the country with Jesse,' she said. 'I was back home over Christmas and I started to really miss all the little things about being in Derry.' But she admitted a move closer to home in the near future wasn't feasible. 'It's impossible to have a career in the pop industry and live in Ireland,' she admitted. 'But when the time is right, I definitely want to return home and buy somewhere really nice to live. I miss being close to my friends and family and Jesse had a great time in Derry.' Nadine wasn't the only Girls Aloud member setting her sights on the Emerald Isle. Perhaps inspired by her inception as the face of Coke Zero in Ireland, Sarah revealed her ultimate dream would see her moving permanently to the country. 'I have actually considered moving to Ireland because I love the country so much,' she conceded. 'It's something I would consider doing in the future. I have a dream of buying a farm somewhere outside Dublin and spending my days in the country – Ireland's rural beauty really seduces me.'

Nadine's relationship with Jesse appeared to be going from strength to strength. She was spending most of her time in LA, and jetting back to London when work commitments with Girls Aloud came calling. 'She walks around with a permanent smile on her face and they are always doing romantic things together,' said Sarah of her bandmate. 'I think it's good for Nadine to be in a serious relationship and I think they will definitely stand the test of time as a couple.' Sarah revealed the band were very fond of their friend's partner, adding, 'We all get on really well with Jesse and he knows most of our songs, so he's got to be a good guy in my book.' But as Nadine spent more time across the Atlantic, the press jumped to the conclusion all was not well in the Girls Aloud ranks. Her father Niall, however, was keen to set the record straight. 'We are here (in LA) at the moment and we can definitely confirm she will be back in the UK soon,' he said. 'She has no intention of leaving Girls Aloud and just wants to spend more time with Jesse. She is very happy.'

Over in LA, Nadine was hanging out with her family and pals – including a certain Miss Natasha Bedingfield. Natasha, who Cheryl once chose as the hypothetical sixth member of Girls Aloud should they be recruiting for an additional member, was filming the video for her comeback single 'I Wanna Have Your Babies' and wanted Nadine to be involved. 'I called her up, like at the last minute, and asked her and she very nicely came along,' said Natasha. So Nadine ended up making a cameo appearance in a club scene in the singer's video, which was released in the UK in April.

Cheryl made the shocking confession that her mum Joan shared her and Ashley's martial home. 'Ashley doesn't do a thing [around the house]. Maybe he'll make me the odd cup of tea, but that's it,' she said, jokingly suggesting martial bliss wasn't all it is cracked up to be. 'Luckily my mum lives with us and she'll do lots of stuff.' Cheryl and Ashley reportedly bought a £3.5 million, seven-bedroom luxury mansion in Surrey – with plenty of room for Chihuahua Buster and presumably, Cheryl's mum. Cheryl even went as far as extending the hand of friendship and the keys to her home to troubled pop princess Britney Spears, who had dramatically shaved off her crowning glory and gone into rehab in California. 'If someone would send her to me, I swear that in four weeks I would have her back to normal.' The pair were rumoured to have pulled the plug on a reported fly-on-the-wall documentary, as they didn't want to fall victim to 'overexposure'.

At the end of January, Girls Aloud joined forces with the Sugababes and a whole host of celebrities for the launch of Comic Relief 2007. Britain's premier girl bands were to record a version of the Aerosmith and Run DMC classic 'Walk This Way' in aid of charity – both groups waived any fees for the release, with all the proceeds going to good causes. Kimberley said, 'It's a fantastic song and will hopefully raise tons of money for people living in really difficult situations here and in Africa.' As part of the Comic Relief fundraisers, Girls Aloud went back to the classroom to film an advert for Walkers crisps under the guidance of 'schoolmaster' Stephen Fry, and with fellow 'pupils' Russell Brand and Gary Lineker, among others. Kimberley visited South Africa with Keisha Buchanan and Heidi Range from the Sugababes for the charity, and found the experience challenging. 'One of the things that I'll remember most from my trip to South

Africa was visiting a family who were being forced from their land, as developers wanted to make way for a large housing development,' she said. 'These people had lived on the land their entire lives, some family members were even buried there. Only a week before we visited, a group of men had come and spray painted their front doors, forcing them out. They were living in fear, and just a stones throw away people were living in luxurious housing – the contrast was just surreal. But there was also hope – we met the head of the family, Joseph who told us how a project funded by money raised from Red Nose Day had stepped in to help the family fight for their land. It definitely puts in perspective what you have at home. The trip has made me realise how fortunate we are here, and we really must do everything we can to help support people less fortunate than ourselves.'

While Kimberley was in Africa for Comic Relief, Cheryl was also doing her bit for charity. Not content with putting the posh shoes she wore in the 'Something Kinda Ooh' video on auction site eBay – raising the grand sum of £363.43 – she had taken part in a celebrity version of *The Apprentice*, filmed in December, and screened in the run up to the big Comic Relief event on 16 March. Working alongside fashion tsar Trinny Woodall – who Cheryl feared would 'criticise her clothes' – football manager Karen Brady, comedienne Jo Brand and actress Maureen Lipman, Cheryl and the team of girls set out to organise a fun fair and raise the most money for charity, against a boys team which included newspaper editor Piers Morgan and former spin doctor for Tony Blair, Alastair Campbell. 'I really enjoyed myself and would do it again,' admitted Cheryl, who appeared on the show getting acquainted with squid innards. 'We raised over a million pounds, which was the main thing.' But the singer conceded the experience was much tougher than appearing on stage in front of an audience of thousands. She said, 'It was much worse than the nerves I get before I go on stage because I was completely outside my comfort zone. When I walked in on the first day I felt intimidated. [But] I knew it was important we raised lots of money for Comic Relief, so I felt a great sense of responsibility.'

After her appearance, Sir Alan Sugar became quite a fan of Mrs Cole's business sense. 'He actually wrote me a note after *The Apprentice* saying if he was to hire anybody, it would be me,' she admitted. 'I was quite open and honest with him. He was trying at the beginning saying I was from a manufactured pop group, and I was like, "Yeah, we are manufactured." I wasn't trying to defend myself. I was just trying to be honest, and I think he respects that.' Cheryl insisted she decided against employing her feminine charm to influence the tycoon. 'I was told it wouldn't be a good idea to flutter my eyelashes at him so I deliberately avoided that as a tactic,' she said. 'Instead I just tried to be professional. You have to be quite savvy [in the music] business to avoid getting ripped off.' Sir Alan was impressed, later telling *Zoo* magazine, 'Cheryl Cole was very impressive. Everyone was expecting this dolly bird, but she showed street smarts, determination, great commitment and a very impressive business acumen. She'll go far, that girl.'

With the praises of Britain's most feared businessman ringing in her ears, Cheryl was allegedly approached to front a new TV series. She had reportedly been asked by *The X Factor* judge and music mogul Simon Cowell to sign up as an adjudicator for his new reality show, *Britain's Got Talent*. But she was quick to deny she would appear on the programme, citing her experience in front of a panel on *Popstars: The Rivals* as the deal-breaker. 'I don't think I can be cruel to anyone, really, and who am I to end their dreams in one go?' she said. 'I wouldn't become a judge. I don't think I would be qualified. Who am I to judge other people? I know people think I'm fiery, but I think I'd be too diplomatic. I know what it is like to be on the receiving end of the criticism.' Another rumour she was keen to dispel was that she was pregnant – pouring cold water on the claims by insisting her stomach wouldn't be as flat as it currently was if she was in fact with child.

Over a year after their riotous cover of Girls Aloud's 'Love Machine', the Arctic Monkeys kept the press on tenterhooks after they claimed they were working with Sarah Harding after she and bandmate Nicola Roberts presented them with the Best Album award at the *NME* Awards in March. Sarah had reportedly said of the band, 'The big tip is we're going to collaborate. I love these boys. They've got a strong future ahead of them.' Frontman Alex Turner told the *NME*, 'I'm finding less and less to say. I'm wilting as a frontman, right, so I'm thinking, third album, we'll just get Sarah Harding to front the band. I'll sing some of the old songs to keep the hardcore happy and then all the new tunes can just be her. Matt Helders [the drummer] and Sarah are in Rockford Studios, that's how it's going to work. Down in Wales for two weeks, two days.' Sarah later credited her remarks to the effects of alcohol. 'Of course we're not doing a bloody album together,' she said. 'I can't believe everyone's making so much of it. Everyone who interviews me know wants to know if we're collaborating. It was a joke. Seriously, the stuff I said at the *NME* Awards was just slightly pissed ranting. The boys joined in on the joke and the next thing I knew it was all over the newspapers.'

The slightly more tangible collaboration with fellow all-girl band the Sugababes was released on 12 March, hitting the number one spot a week later. The video showed each band on separate sides of a dividing wall, all glammed up and indulging in a bit of destructive behaviour, hitting the wall willy-nilly with guitars and the like before walking down two separate catwalks for each of the two bands, with a suspended microphone contributing to a sing-off between the Girls and the 'Babes. As befitting a Comic Relief single, a slew of celebrities appear in the video; Graham Norton, Davina McCall and Ruby Wax are among those who strut their stuff during the closing words of the song. The single was Girls Aloud's 15th top ten hit and their fifth cover version – posting on the Girls Aloud website, Sarah promised 'no more covers' on the forthcoming fifth album.

The world of celebrity was shocked when Jesse was

admitted to rehab in the middle of March; not least his girlfriend Nadine. The pair had appeared in a lavish 12-page shoot for *OK!* Magazine published the same week, shot on location in Hawaii. After a four-day bender in LA, which saw him thrown out of the swanky Mondrian Hotel for alleged abusive drunken behaviour, he entered the Promises Centre in Malibu, California – where Britney Spears had spent her time in rehab earlier in the year. A statement issued by the actor's spokesperson read, 'On Monday [19 March], Jesse Metcalfe entered a rehab facility to deal with alcohol issues. He realised he had a problem and was anxious to deal with it immediately. The actor hopes that the media will allow him the privacy to deal properly with his treatment.'

Nadine was understandably upset, but glad Jesse had faced up to the problem, and vowed to stand by him. 'Jesse is getting help,' she said. 'I'm just glad he has realised he couldn't go on the way he was. It was hurting me to see him do that to himself. I'm going to be there for him and do all I can to help but at the end of the day, Jesse has to make the decision to stop on his own.' Nadine's dad Niall, who had met the actor on many occasions, often playing host to the star in the Coyle family home, spoke of his shock at the turn of events. 'We saw Jesse regularly when we were in the US, and we often thought he drank less than us. Maybe he was trying to hide the fact that he had a problem from the people he cares about. Nadine is devastated this has happened and blames herself.' But he insisted the pair were staying together as a couple, with Nadine spending hours on the phone with Jesse supporting him. 'She will be there for him while he goes through the programme and will be there when he comes out,' he added.

Shampoo firm Sunsilk announced they had signed a one-year deal with Girls Aloud to promote a new range of products, with each girl fronting a different shampoo and conditioner. The deal, which saw the girls land an estimated £250,000 each, also brought sponsorship for the band's forthcoming greatest hits tour. A spokesperson for the company said, 'This is the first time we have done anything on this scale. We're very pleased to be working with Girls Aloud.' As the tour approached, the band was getting more excited about the performances ahead of them.

But amid the euphoria and anticipation of a month on the road during the 16-date tour, bad news was to befall Nadine. Jesse was spotted cosying up to an unidentified brunette following his spell in rehab. The end was nigh, after nearly 15 months together, and Nadine quite rightly gave him the boot. 'It's over between me and Jesse,' she admitted. 'I'm not the kind of girl to put up with nonsense like that. I'll meet the right person when the time is right. I'm disappointed but what can you do? There's no point in hanging on when it gets to this stage.'

Meanwhile, Cheryl was causing a few sparks of jealousy to fly in the Cole household when she confessed to having a crush on husband Ashley's boss, Chelsea manager Jose Mourinho. 'He has definitely got something about him. He has a presence and a lot of charisma, and I think everybody loves a little bit of bad-boy arrogance. He's stylish and a little bit older, so yes, I've got a twinkle in my eye for him.'

After Nadine and Jesse's break up, Nadine threw herself into her work with the band. She told reporters, 'I'm busy doing work with Girls Aloud, so I have plenty going on.' In May, the groups found time in their busy schedule to film a cameo stint in a remake of the *St Trinian's* movie with Rupert Everett. Dressed in school uniforms, Kimberley, Nadine, Cheryl, Nicola and Sarah filmed their parts over two days in Ealing studios and on location in Henley-on-Thames, Oxfordshire. Cheryl explained, 'We did two days filming. It's only a small part – we're supposed to be the St Trinian's school band. It was really good fun. I thought it was going to be hard work but it wasn't. We just really enjoyed ourselves. We had a new song, The St Trinian's Song, and we just had to sing along with a crowd of kids.'

With only days to go before the tour, the girls were excited about the prospect of playing to thousands of their fans, beginning with a gig in Newcastle on 14 May and ending in Belfast on 2 June. 'It's huge,' said Cheryl of the planned spectacle, without even a whiff of hyperbole. 'It's the biggest show to date, our greatest hits, all our career so far rounded up in one show. If you're a Girls Aloud fan you're going to wet your pants. I don't want to give too much away but I got goosebumps just watching our dancers going through the motions. My hairs were standing up on the back of my neck.'

CHAPTER 19

Love/Hate

ALMOST AS SOON as Girls Aloud were formed in November 2002, the haters and a whole host of doubting Thomases were lining up to take their shots at the newest group on the block. While many established pop stars expressed their concern for a reality TV-formed outfit, there were plenty of other celebrities getting on the wrong side of the group. Let's take a look at Girls Aloud's showbiz rivalries over the years – and my, do these girls pull no punches.

GIRLS ALOUD VS ONE TRUE VOICE FEATURING PETE WATERMAN

It began as some reality TV camaraderie between Pete Waterman's vocal harmony group One True Voice and Louis Walsh's fabulous feisty females. Despite undergoing the same arduous process to eventually form a band, the race for the Christmas number one spot was acrimonious. Pete wasn't too complimentary about the girls' singing talents. 'What I couldn't get my head round was that you all watched the same programme as me, but then everyone is telling me the girls are brilliant,' said a flummoxed Pete. 'The public know these girls can't sing, so what am I missing? I didn't go down the marketing route because I was stupid enough to believe in talent. If Girls Aloud are the most exciting thing in pop at the moment, then God help us.' Pete also famously claimed the band hadn't sung on the 'Sound Of The Underground' single – a claim which was later refuted.

Keith, Anton, Jamie, Matt and Daniel also threw their tuppence-worth into the Arena of Jealously, calling the girls 'tarts' for their sexy video shoot style. 'We thought they were our friends and now they've taken it to a personal level,' said Cheryl. 'They've called us tarts and said we can't sing or dance. It's taken it beyond a joke but we're not going to sink that low. We wish them all the best. I don't know why they've taken it to this extent. They're insulting all the people who voted for us to be in the band so they're not doing themselves any favours.' The Geordie lass was keen to point out the boys weren't a hit with one of pop's most prolific audiences – gay men. She explains, 'We went to a gay club in London and it was fantastic. They were chanting "Number One!" to the girls and the boys weren't too happy. If they can't even sell themselves to gay men, well, it says it all, really.' G-A-Y promoter Jeremy Joseph added it was the girls who triumphed in the battle of the pop newbies. 'The girls walked it,' he said. 'Before the gig the general vibe was that most of the crowds had come down for the boys. But after Girls Aloud's amazing stage show everyone seemed to change their mind and said they'd be backing the girls.'

When One True Voice fell on troubled times, Nadine admitted, 'It feels good. They had to eat serious humble pie because they were sure they were going to get to number one. We hadn't slagged them at all but they were really crafty. Daniel phoned me and said, "Please don't slag us off." But they ripped us to shreds, saying we were dressing like tarts in the video. We were shocked that they were so two-faced. It's kind of gone bad for them. It's unfortunate but they did have attitude and air about them. They turned a bit arrogant.'

Unsurprisingly, Girls Aloud had the last laugh when in August 2003, just nine months after their formation, One True Voice announced their intentions to split. The words of Keith Semple in December 2002 came back to haunt them: 'If they get the No.1, then good luck to them – because they won't be around for much longer after that.' Keith, take note. Fifteen singles and four albums later, Kimberley, Cheryl, Nicola, Sarah and Nadine are still sashaying their way up the pop charts. One True Voice are not.

GIRLS ALOUD VS SIMON COWELL

High-waisted trouser fan and full-time music mogul Simon Cowell strongly criticised Cheryl Tweedy and her

Girls Aloud bandmates on the back of a new series of *Pop Idol*. Wheeling out yet another controversial soundbite, Simon questioned Cheryl's singing ability at the launch of the new *Idol* series. He said, 'I think the Geordie girl Cheryl is terrible. I saw her last audition. She didn't sing a note in tune.' The band got into hot water by alleging the crop of wannabes for the 2003 series of *Pop Idol* 'weren't as good' as in previous years, so Simon later invited the five starlets to sing live on the series to prove they had talent, but the girls politely declined his request. Simon asked Girls Aloud to 'prove themselves', but Sarah replied, 'We already have.' Despite the eventual *Pop Idol* winner, Michelle McManus fading into relative obscurity, Girls Aloud went – and continue to go – from strength to strength with their high-heeled attack on the music industry.

Any musical hatchets between the outspoken ladies and Cowell were buried in early 2007 when Cheryl was rumoured to have been asked to be a judge on TV talent show *Britain's Got Talent*... headed up by Mr Cowell himself. Despite turning the role down, all past differences were forgotten in an instant, and Cheryl now gushes about the acid-tongued music supremo. 'I know what it is like to be on the receiving end of the criticism,' she says. 'I love Simon Cowell though, I think he has a good heart – he really is a pussy cat.'

NICOLA ROBERTS VS MATT FROM BUSTED

Another inter-pop tiff was brewing for Girls Aloud not long after they came to prominence at the end of 2002.

Matt Willis, one third of boy-pop rockers Busted intimated in a magazine interview that Nicola was 'a rude ginger bitch' because she had ignored him at an event. Manager Louis Walsh even stepped into the fray, barring the Busted boys from seeing the band after Matt's rude remarks. Matt said of Louis, 'He was really rude and ignorant to us. He is well on my hit list. We wanted to speak to the girls and say hello but he wouldn't let us near them. As far as Louis Walsh goes, if you say clock and take out the L, that's what he is.' Nicola plotted her revenge, and appeared on stage at a gig in London's G-A-Y club with 'I'm a rude ginger bitch...bothered' emblazoned on her rear as a clear response to Willis' comments. 'I was just having a bit of fun, showing we have attitude,' explained Nicola. 'Matt acted like a silly little boy. He phoned up a magazine and moaned how I'd been rude to him – a total lie.'

But the disharmony wasn't to last long, with Willis insisting it wasn't Nicola he didn't like, it was Girls Aloud's entourage: 'I don't actually have a problem with Nicola anymore. I'm over that. It's her management. I actually think Girls Aloud are gonna do quite well.'

GIRLS ALOUD VS SIMON AMSTELL AND MIQUITA OLIVER

'I'd much rather say something stupid or offensive than not say anything and feel a bit weak.' So said former *Popworld* host Simon Amstell, not one for mincing his words. 'When I watch an interview back, I always regret an unasked question. Apparently I recently upset Girls

Aloud. I can live with that.' Famed for its irreverent humour, Girls Aloud aren't big fans of music show *Popworld*. Curly-haired presenter Amstell ignited a full-scale handbags at dawn war between himself and the quintet, describing them as 'vile'. Not long after Cheryl's incident with a nightclub's lavatory attendant, the infamously deadpan Amstell asked how fellow toilet-goers react when they see Cheryl in the loo. Needless to say, the girls were not amused. But it wasn't just Amstell they cultivated a dislike for – it was co-host Miquita Oliver too.

'Oh God, those two knobs!' said Kimberley. 'Pair of idiots. They have a go at us every time they get the chance.' Nicola branded Oliver as 'looking like she doesn't wash' and opined that Amstell was 'a right horrible bitchy old queen who needs his hair-cutting'. But the last word is reserved for Cheryl, who offered up a psychoanalytical analysis of *Never Mind The Buzzcocks* host Amstell's behaviour. 'I think he's one of those people who was bullied at school. You can tell by the way he tries to have a go at people now. I don't think he's a happy person. I think he thinks slagging people off is a way to make friends. You know the type. They slagged us off when we first started and said we wouldn't be around for five minutes. It hurt then, because we didn't know that we would be. But here we are, That's my answer to them, really. You think you can do something better, go and do it.'

GIRLS ALOUD VS DANNII MINOGUE

Despite sharing a link through the pop-tinged music of production supremo Brian Higgins and Xenomania,

Girls Aloud and Dannii Minogue have exchanged acid-tongued insults. The band expressed their disdain for what they called Minogue's 'less-than-natural' appearance, and reckoned she'd have more success with the opposite sex if she refrained from going under the knife. Cheryl said, 'I think Dannii Minogue should get all her plastic surgery reduced. She doesn't look natural. I don't think men find her attractive.' The younger Minogue sister was less than impressed with the girl's remarks, but the parties were forced to face each other often during the summer of 2003, when they shared the billing at countless poptastic gigs.

Dannii's right to reply was thus, singling out Nicola for criticism – but decided to brand the entire band 'a bunch of chavs'. 'The bitchiest are Girls Aloud – I think the redhead's got it in for me,' she said. 'After a show in Scotland, Nicola was saying vile stuff about me. I saw her at last year's Disney Awards and just smiled. I mean, the punch-ups, going to court... I don't want to get involved – I'm no Chav.'

GIRLS ALOUD VS ALL SAINTS

When late Nineties pop combo All Saints settled their differences after a well-documented fall out between bandmembers Shaznay Lewis, Melanie Blatt, and the sisters Appleton, Natalie and Nicole, they relaunched their musical career with comeback single 'Rock Steady', hoping to emulate Take That's remarkably successful Second Coming. Kimberley said, 'Good luck to them, I hope they stay friends this time.' But Girls

Aloud were not amused. 'The new All Saints sound just sounds like us. They must have looked at what's working at the moment and thought, 'We'll go that way', but the whole reuniting band thing at the moment is driving me insane.'

During an interview with the *Guardian*, the Girls Aloud collective took time out to vocalise their feelings towards their girl band rivals, adding a satirical slant to All Saint hit 'Never Ever' through the medium of song: 'A few questions that we need to know/ Is it because you needed the dough?/ We need to know why you came back/ With such a blatant Girls Aloud track/ Is it coz we've had more hits than The Supremes/ You couldn't do that in your fuckin' dreams/ Either way you're going out of your mind/ For ever getting back together after all this time. . . SUCKERS!!!!'

All Saints hit back, with Blatt saying of the comparison, 'That's so true, because 'Jump (For My Love)' is so where I wanna be. We could only aspire and dream to be like them. Hopefully, one day we will achieve that. For now we will just have to make do with copying them.' Nicole insightfully believed the only common reference point between the two bands was their gender: 'We all have vaginas, that's as familiar as it gets.' Shaznay stepped into the row, insisting Girls Aloud had better beware when they next would have a face to face encounter with All Saints. 'We say what we want,' she said. 'As long as we stand true and say what we really believe, it's fine. If you say things about people for any other reason you have to be careful because you will bump into them. So you'd better mean what you say. It's not cockiness – it's maturity.'

Ever the peacemaker, Sarah attempted to end the row by giving an explanation for it all – and admitted she had even been sharing a few beers with All Saints star Natalie: 'It's all bollocks. It was taken out of proportion, twisted, and they retaliated. I actually had a drink with Natalie Appleton and Liam Gallagher the other week as we have a mutual friend – everything is fine, honestly.'

GIRLS ALOUD VS CHARLOTTE CHURCH

Charlotte Church's change of musical direction for her sixth album caused a bit of a stir in the pop world – the former *Voice Of An Angel* had abandoned her classical roots in favour of recording some pop belters for *Tissues And Issues*. The move opened a heated debate among music lovers – not least Girls Aloud. In an interview with Radio 1, Cheryl said she'd 'let Charlotte get on with using their old sound'. Church was quick to respond, challenging Cheryl to a sing-off. 'You get the likes of Cheryl friggin' Tweedy from Girls Aloud saying that 'Crazy Chick' was a Girls Aloud-style song,' she said, 'but that was okay, I could have their old style because they're working on a new style. I thought, "Love, as soon as you can fucking sing Ave Maria, then you can have a go." That girl should piss off and go get a hobby. I mean, it takes more than that to get to me. I used to love Girls Aloud, but not any more after that one. Girls Aloud wouldn't be able to sing 'Crazy Chick' if they possibly tried. They just don't have the range, darling. And when they've sold as many records as me, then they can comment.' Nadine stepped in, saying, 'She can keep saying things about us as long as she wants but we're not bothered. She's got no vocal style – anybody can sing the songs the way she does. There's nothing special there.'

As the months went on, the comments got cattier, with Cheryl calling the Welsh singer 'a nasty little piece of work with a fat head,' and deeming her advert for Walker's crisps 'very appropriate' because it saw her 'stuffing her face'. Church's boyfriend, Welsh rugby international Gavin Henson also felt the sting of Cheryl's tongue: 'I don't know who her and her scabby boyfriend think they are. He's a posing idiot who looks like a girl. And she's not even gorgeous.' Church then threatened to beat up Cheryl over the spat: 'First of all it was quite funny, but now it's just pathetic and I'm going to knock her out if I ever see her.'

But like all well-behaved ladies, the pair decided to put the past behind them and call a truce. Cheryl blamed the vitriol on a misunderstanding, 'Someone asked me if I was devastated we hadn't had a chance to record 'Crazy Chick'. I just felt like it was an insult, because we had made good records. I said 'We're moving on now, so if Charlotte wants to do that sound she can.' Then she started ranting and raving. We've yet to kiss and make up, but I'm open to the idea.' Church too admitted she was 'bored' with the spat, even insinuating she was open to the idea of inviting her arch enemy onto her

Channel 4 chat show, *The Charlotte Church Show*, and wished her all the best for the future. 'As for Cheryl, why not? I'm bored of our feud,' she said. 'She looked lovely at her wedding and I've never actually met her. I hope she's really happy.'

GIRLS ALOUD VS BOY GEORGE

The girls felt the wrath of legendary Culture Club frontman and DJ Boy George at the Vodafone Live! awards in 2006. The star, famed for his acerbic remarks about fellow singers – including musical stalwarts Sir Elton John and Madonna – called the group 'moany' and not up to scratch when it comes to singing live. He said, 'I wish Girls Aloud would stop moaning – it's all they do. There are so many better live acts.' But the band was quick to respond to the jibes, although they didn't quite 'understand his problem'. 'I knew George didn't like us from the moment we walked into the room,' admits Kimberley. 'Where was he when we performed last? Oh yeah, he was picking up dog shit in New York,' said Sarah, in reference to Boy George's community service carried out in the Big Apple. Cheryl believed the row came down to cosmetic know-how, as Boy George is well known for his flamboyant facial decoration and bizarre black-painted neck: 'He's just furious that we've got a better make-up artist, [and is] bitter that he's not succeeding and we are', she said. Sarah added, 'And that we don't need all that shading that he does to hide his three chins.'

GIRLS ALOUD VS PETER ANDRE AND JORDAN

Following the pink-filled wedding of Jordan (AKA Katie Price) and her Prince Charming Peter Andre in 2005 at which Sarah was a bridesmaid, Cheryl allegedly expressed interest in the couple's venue of choice, Highclere Castle, as a potential location for her and fiancé Ashley Cole's nuptials the following summer. But when she realised the posh venue had been the scene of Jordan's big day, she reportedly reassessed her options. If tabloid reports are to be believed, she decided to avoid the place like the plague; despite citing the location as her wedding venue in a purposeful press-directed red herring. Former pop star Andre was not amused, as when the Coles' big day finally came around, he believed it bore more than just a passing resemblance to his wedding the previous year. He said, 'Cheryl has allegedly said having a horse and carriage is tacky and there's no way she'd get married where Katie and I got married. But parts of their wedding were similar to ours. She shouldn't be bitchy. It doesn't suit her.'

GIRLS ALOUD VS LILY ALLEN

It all started when the doyenne of the British music scene, Lily Allen, penned a song entitled 'Cheryl Tweedy', which found itself as the B-side to her number one single 'Smile'. Professing through the lyrics she 'wished she looked like Cheryl Tweedy', the press was quick to find out what the lady in question thought of the track. Cheryl said, 'I'm really flattered Lily's written a track about me. But I don't know why she sings about wanting to be as pretty as me as she looks stunning. I'd like to look like her. I love her single and the way she wears trainers with gorgeous dresses. It's about time we had a really cool British girl out there on the music scene.' Looking at the lyrics more closely, it was clear the song wasn't as straightforward as Cheryl had been led to believe. The biggest blow, however, was yet to come, when Allen conceded the track was far from what it seemed. 'I don't want to look like Cheryl Tweedy. It's tongue in cheek, it's meant to be ironic. I don't have anything against her as I human being, but I think the portrayal of her being the right thing for kids to look up to is wrong. It was a joke that not many people got. Of course nobody wants to look like Cheryl, they just think they do.' Adding insult to injury, the singer then dubbed Cheryl and husband Ashley 'horrendous'.

Cheryl's Girls Aloud bandmates stepped into the fray. Kimberley conceded she enjoyed Lily's *Smile* and *LDN*, but was no longer impressed by her personality: 'I don't really like her as a person.' Nicola, however, was the most irked by Allen and her nasty comments and made her feelings towards the songstress known. 'Lily was saying she liked me because I was moody and not that pretty,' she explains. 'I really appreciated her when she first came out – she was a breath of fresh air. But now I think, well, fuck her,' later branding her a 'chick with a dick'.

CHERYL TWEEDY VS THE PUSSYCAT DOLLS

Cheryl admitted she enjoyed the hits of American all-singing, all-dancing and fellow all-girl troupe The Pussycat Dolls, but didn't like their penchant for releasing a seemingly never-ending stream of singles from their 2005 album PCD – half the tracklisting in total. Cheryl conceded she didn't think much of frontwoman Nicole Scherzinger, deeming her 'not as talented' as her US chanteuse contemporaries in light of the singer's attempts to go solo. She said, 'I like their music but they've hammered the album, this is like their 20th single off it. I don't think [lead singer Nicole could [cut it solo]. You've got the likes of Beyoncé, Britney and Christina. I don't think she stands out as amazing. She hasn't got what Christina's got.'

GIRLS ALOUD VS KAISER CHIEFS

British indie darlings the Kaiser Chiefs were none too pleased when Girls Aloud covered their hit 'I Predict A Riot' on their 2006 *Chemistry* tour. The girls sang the tune in their own inimitable style, but made one fatal error – they changed the lyrics. Not wanting to corrupt any young fans in the audience, they swapped the words 'borrow a pound for a condom' for 'borrowed a pound for a phone call'. The money-lending high jinks infuriated Kaiser Chiefs frontman Ricky Wilson, who admitted that he didn't mind the cover version, but wasn't best pleased they altered the songwords. 'I don't give a shit if they don't change the words,' he said. 'But they did change the words.' He admitted he much preferred Lily Allen's version of his song, recorded with superstar producer Mark Ronson: 'Lily Allen asked permission. Girls Aloud didn't – and they changed the words. It's embarrassing.' And Wilson threatened to get his own back in an act of retaliation: 'I'm gonna cover a Girls Aloud song and change all their words, but make them really filthy.' Rockers Kasabian added their slant to the riotous debacle, adding that Girls Aloud shouldn't have been allowed on the bill at the V Festival for their sins. Guitarist Serge Pizzorno said, 'Girls Aloud should be nowhere near that festival. I'd have been devastated if they'd done one of our songs.'

GIRLS ALOUD VS MELANIE C

Poor Girls Aloud. Five girls, brilliant mould-breaking pop tunes; they were the ready-made successors to the Spice Girls. But Melanie C, now free of her Sporty Spice moniker, had other ideas. The girls had idolised the band during their formative years and were delighted when manager Louis Walsh dubbed them 'the Spice Girls with personalities' – Mel retorted with, 'Well, when they rack up 37 million albums worldwide, come back and talk to me.'

Her scathing comments didn't end there. While she conceded Girls Aloud were good, she opined they would 'never be the next Spice Girls'. She said, 'It is frustrating at times when I see some acts that are top of the charts,' Mel retorted, 'but the fact is I was there for years with the girls and now it's their turn. There's no doubt Girls

Aloud are absolute babes, but to be honest, they always look miserable. They're good, but they'll never be the next Spice Girls. We had something special that they'll never emulate.'

Cheryl put the comments down to a publicity stunt. 'When we were at primary school we were inspired by the Spice Girls. It's sad she has to bitch about us.'

GIRLS ALOUD VS PETE DOHERTY

Despite hanging off the arm of one of the world's most sought-after women, Girls Aloud didn't see the point of former Libertines man Pete Doherty. Kate Moss' beau or not, the Babyshambles frontman's history of drug abuse and musical talent were singled out for the wrath of the girls, who branded him 'a junkie idiot'. Kimberley said, 'I guess that if you like brown teeth and mouldy fingers, he's your guy,' while Cheryl attacked him for bringing heroin onto a higher platform in the public psyche. 'That junkie idiot,' she said. 'The problem I have with him is that I've lost friends to heroin and I just don't get the idea of glorifying it. I think it's disgusting. There are enough drug problems without him being in the public eye and sticking needles in his arms in the press. If he kicks his habit, he'll be a lot more respected.'

While Sarah dubbed Doherty 'very creative', it was Nadine who threw down the musical gauntlet, challenging Doherty to a style-swapping contest. She said, 'He's supposed to be this musical genius, but has anyone heard him sing? I've heard a Babyshambles album and it was like, "What am I listening to?" We could make a record that sounded like that, but could he make one that sounded like us?'

But just as the Girls Aloud-dissing rumpus appeared to be in full swing, the flipside of fame became apparent – do your job well and the critics will be lining up to declare their undying love.

Martin Talbot of industry bible *Music Week* believes the girls' appeal lies in their reputation as a feisty fivesome. 'Only one or two pop acts ever really have a cutting edge to them – Girls Aloud definitely do,' he says. 'One thing that gives them more cachet, more cool, is the fact that they're not squeaky clean, not just another S Club 7, Westlife or whatever. If the poppy kids like to dress up like them, so those into the more dangerous, rock'n'roll side of things would probably like to spend and evening in a bar with them. They've got an edge. They're unpredictable.'

Nicola thinks things have come full circle and knows it's now cool to like the band. 'It was never cool to like Girls Aloud because of the whole reality TV thing,' she says. 'But now we've been around so long, I'd like to think people respect the fact we are one of the only reality bands still around – not even so much reality bands – pop bands in general.' The girls' longevity is testament to their talent and Xenomania's knack of matchmaking Girls Aloud with top notch pop tunes – a kind of custom tailoring which makes it perfectly clear tracks like 'Something Kinda Ooh' or 'Biology' just wouldn't sit well on any other artists. Girls Aloud's constant deference to producer Brian Higgins and songwriter Miranda Cooper is refreshing; in an age of credible acts, Girls Aloud embrace their 'manufactured band' tag and proudly flaunt it in the face of whoever is looking... letting their music speak for itself. As Nicola quite rightly pointed out, 'It's not like we're the only pop band around who auditioned for their places.' 'We don't write our own songs and we don't have any right to say we want to be part of pop history, but we have changed the rules in what you can do in a pop band,' opines Cheryl.

Ever since the birth of Girls Aloud, serious music critics have been lining up to praise the band – Nicola in particular was soon outed as the journalists' favourite. Online magazine *Stylus*, famed for its stinging put downs of anything remotely resembling chart pop, were singing the girls' praises after the release of *What Will The Neighbours Say?*: 'Every action is executed with the intention of reaffirming their status as The Greatest Pop Group In The Entire Fucking World.' The hallelujahs in praise of, as Cheryl put it, 'pop at its best', certainly didn't stop there, with traditionally militant indie magazines hopping on the Girls Aloud gospel train. Cheryl says, 'To hear the likes of *NME*, who are a highly credible magazine that love to hate pop, writing good things about our music is unheard of.' Sarah believes the reason behind their success is their musical bravado, which lets them stick two fingers up at the boundaries of pop. 'We have never done the kind of pop that people expect girl bands to do,' she says. 'It's not teen pop. It's always been grown up. Just because we're a girl band, people used to just think we made shit pop records and it's only now over the past year that we have noticed a change with people saying how much they liked out songs and how it was cool to say you liked Girls Aloud.'

The bright young things of the media world got together in late 2006 and produced a Girls Aloud fanzine. No other pop band could incite such passion within such a traditionally fickle profession. *Heat* editor Mark Frith filled a page explaining why Nicola is 'Britain's Finest Pop Star', while music critic Alexis Petridis named the group 'The Greatest Rock And Roll Band In The World.' High praise indeed. But before Girls Aloud begin taking themselves far too seriously, they once again remind the world that pop isn't about bringing about any kind of revolution or high-brow happening.

'Music is just music,' says Nadine. 'It's wonderful, but it's not going to change the world. It's not going to bring world peace, it's not going to do anything serious. It's just entertainment – get over it!'

Epilogue

WITH THEIR BIGGEST ever tour on the cards and work on their fifth album afoot, the girls are going from strength to strength after nearly five years together – and insist they're not about to split. Posting on the band's website, Sarah wrote, 'Don't believe the ridiculous story about us splitting up. As you know by now, some people just can't stop making stories up out of nothing.' In the time the girls have been together, since that fateful day in November 2002, tales of the collapse of pop's greatest hope have darkened the pages of many a gossip column – all of which have proved to be unfounded. 'There's been this rumour ever since we got together,' says Cheryl. 'I swear it's just one journalist who does the same story every other week. He clearly hasn't got anything to write about. We're not going anywhere. Get used to it!'

But the girls are stoical about the inevitable – they are all very much aware their pop path as a quintet won't last forever. Pragmatic Cheryl knows Girls Aloud may run its course sooner rather than later: 'I think it would be foolish to think that people haven't thought about what they want to do after the band. Realistically, how long have we got? Another few years if that?' Sarah adds, 'It's not going to last forever and we all acknowledge that. Being a girl band or a boy band, you only have so long on your shelf life. [But] I reckon we'll be around for a while. People always ask us if any of us will make it as a solo artist when we split, but I don't think it's fair to speculate on something like that, because we're all great friends and the future is bright.'

Each of the girls has spoken of their hopes and dreams after Girls Aloud is no more. 'In an ideal world, after the band I'd like to start a family, but at the same time I want to secure my future,' says Cheryl. 'Where I want to be is far from where I am at the minute, so I think I'll work for another couple of years before I start a family.' Sarah has recently been pursuing acting roles, with a part in gangster movie *Bad Day,* but reckons she'd make a good entrepreneur somewhere along the line. 'I'd like to own my own business at some stage in the future and call all the shots,' she says. 'I have a good head for that kind of thing and it would be great to fall back on that whenever my career in the music business finishes.' Kimberley has expressed an interest in a return to acting and dancing post-Girls Aloud, while the band's most prolific songwriter Nicola may continue to pen tracks long after her Girls Aloud days are over – and Louis Walsh has made no secret of the fact he wants to sign Nadine as a solo artist when Girls Aloud ends.

When Girls Aloud is no more, rest assured there will be no exits under a cloud à la Geri, Brian or Robbie – once one member goes, they all go. 'From the start,' explains Cheryl, 'We said if anyone's really unhappy or if the band goes really drastically downhill and nobody's buying the records, then we'll make a decision as a band to end it, not that somebody leaves or quits and then starts slagging each other off in our autobiographies and all that rubbish.' Kimberley adds, 'I would really love to think that we could possibly be the one and only band that ended without anyone leaving first. With no backstabbing. It's always like Westlife or Take That.'

With their slew of record breaking success and a run of top ten hits surpassing that of The Supremes, Girls Aloud are a once-in-a-lifetime phenomenon. It may be only a matter of time until Kimberley, Cheryl, Nadine, Nicola and Sarah go their separate ways, but for now, they're well and truly at the top of the pop game and hope to stay there for a little while longer. They are one of the few survivors in the tempestuous tide of pop – their ability to adapt over the years thanks to a combination of Xenomania's gold dust and their own feisty yet lovable demeanour has proved to be the secret to their staying power. Cheryl perfectly describes the band thusly, 'I just hope that when they make future telly programmes about pop history, we're there as the band who changed everything in 2002.'

Discography

SINGLES		
Title	**Release Date**	**Highest UK chart position**
Sound Of The Underground	16/12/02	1
No Good Advice	12/05/03	2
Life Got Cold	18/08/03	3
Jump	17/11/03	2
The Show	28/06/04	2
Love Machine	13/09/04	2
I'll Stand By You	15/11/04	1
Wake Me Up	21/02/05	4
Long Hot Summer	22/08/05	7
Biology	14/11/05	4
See The Day	05/12/05	9
Whole Lotta History	13/03/06	6
Something Kinda Ooh	23/10/06	3
I Think We're Alone Now	18/12/06	4
Walk This Way	12/03/07	1

girls aloud

ALBUMS		
Title	**Release Date**	**Copies Sold**
Sound Of The Underground	2003	340,000 Platinum
What will the Neighbours Say?	2004	570,000 Double Platinum
Chemistry	2005	360,000 Platinum
The Sound OF Girls Aloud	2006	815,000 Triple Platinum